Papers on Residential Work

Disturbed Children

Edited by Robert J. N. Tod MA, AAPSW

With a foreword by the late Dr D. W. Winnicott, MA, FRCP, MRCS
Honorary Consulting Physician, Paddington Green Children's Hospital
President, British Psychoanalytical Society

Longman

LONGMAN GROUP LIMITED
London
Associated companies, branches and representatives throughout the world

© *Longman Group Limited* 1968

First published 1968
Second impression 1969
Third impression 1973

ISBN 0 582 42853 X

*Set in Monotype Garamond type
and printed in
Hong Kong by Wing Tai Cheung Printing Co. Ltd.*

Contents

Contents

Foreword

I wish to commend this book not only to those engaged in residential work with children but also, and especially, to students of advanced and specialized residential courses. Books of this kind are needed just now when the focus of immediate developments in social work training is just here, in the better understanding and in the teaching of the principles of care of disturbed children in residential settings.

The study of children in foster homes has been carried a long way, and the time is now ripe for more attention to be given to residential work. Good work is all the time being done in residential homes, and a vast experience has been gained, but not perhaps collected together and structured into a theoretical statement. But a working theory is necessary if the plan is to be carried through whereby every residential worker will be recognized as doing one variety of social work.

The authors of these articles fully recognize the fact that children in boarding establishments are in fact disturbed children, adversely affected not only by their antecedent experiences but also by the simple fact of being away from home. Life is difficult enough for all children, so that if they are to reach the various developmental phases at appropriate ages they need special environmental provision, which usually they do get. They are dependent, but they are cared for by dependable people, that is, by people who feel responsible for them and love them. When the environment fails, however, a child is thrown back on his or her own resources, and it is but seldom that this works, or works well, and in any case there results a more or less gross interference with the processes of emotional and personality growth. Those who are caring for children in homes are dealing with disturbed children, even when it is only a temporary state of affairs that has produced this need; and often the child has had to be placed because of a serious or disastrous environmental defect, such as the estrangement of parents who had seemed to be rock-firm. Those who take over responsibility for children need more than intuition, understanding and common sense, however valuable these qualities may be as a foundation. They need to be able to observe, to stand aside, to think things out, and to have a backbone of theory on which to hang whatever they find.

In this book, students and workers in residential homes will find help as they try to sort out, one from another, the good and the bad things that are inherent in this highly specialized application of the principles of child care. I feel that Mr Tod has made a good choice of articles, and that his sparse editorial comments give the reader orientation without offering distraction from the individual authors' specific contributions.

D. W. Winnicott

Acknowledgements

I would like to acknowledge with thanks permission to reproduce articles in this book to the following journals and authors:

The American Journal of Orthopsychiatry, 1790 Broadway, New York, N.Y. 10019 U.S.A. and Miss Mary J. Riley for no. 11. Copyright, the American Orthopsychiatric Association, Inc. Reproduced by permission.

Case Conference, 5 Sudbury Gardens, Croydon, Surrey and Prof. E. J. Anthony and Dr F. Bodman respectively for no. 10 and no. 3.

Child Care: The Quarterly Review of the National Council of Voluntary Child Care Organizations, 85 Highbury Park, London, N.5, and Mrs C. Winnicott for no. 7.

Child Welfare, The Child Welfare League of America Inc., 44 East 23 Street, New York, N.Y. 10010, U.S.A. and Dr Elliot Studt, Mr S. Adessa and Miss Laatsch, and Mr D. Farrington, Dr W. Shelton and Mr J. R. McKay respectively for no. 1, no. 5 and no. 9.

Children, The Children's Bureau, The United States Department of Health, Education and Welfare, Welfare Administration, Washington D.C. 20201, U.S.A. and Mr S. Z. Moss for no. 4.

The Howard Journal, 6 Endsleigh Street, London, W.C.1 and Dr M. Franklin for no. 2.

The New Era in Home and School, Yew Tree Cottage, Roundabouts, Five Ashes, Mayfield, Sussex and Mrs B. E. Dockar-Drysdale for no. 8.

The Residential Child Care Association, Earlsfield House, 1, Swaffield Road, S.W.18 and Mrs B. E. Dockar-Drysdale for no. 6.

R.J.N.T.

Introduction

This is the second of two books of collected articles which have
appeared in English or in American periodicals in recent years.
The previous book entitled *Papers on Residential Work: Children in
Care* was concerned with deprived children who were able to
respond to family-type care from people who saw their role as
temporary parent-representatives and could also understand and
tolerate some of the difficult behaviour that unhappy children
show. The present book is directed to the care and treatment of
disturbed children whose previous experience of parent figures has
been so painful or so confusing that they initially respond to
ordinary affection with suspicion or with hostility. Such children
can be profoundly disturbing to our own emotional balance, as
they threaten our hard won adjustment to our own immature
selves and provoke us into being either emotionally over-involved
or harshly rejecting.

   In the past a few inspired individuals have intuitively penetrated
to the private world of such children and provided them with an
acceptable pattern of adult identification. The unconscious nature
of their understanding, however, based as it might be on some
shared and unverbalized fantasy, has made it difficult for them to
report or describe their methods in any systematic way. Such
pioneers have inspired disciples rather than formulated theories. It
is not in question that sensitivity, intuition and imagination are an
essential base for work with disturbed children, but on this base
needs to be built systematic knowledge of the causes of children's
disturbance and of the unconscious meaning of symptomatic
behaviour. Further, workers with maladjusted children should be
involved in a continuous study and examination of their own

techniques of care and treatment. In short what is urgently needed is a rationale of residential care and treatment of deprived and disturbed children.

As a contribution towards such a rationale of residential treatment the articles that follow have been chosen. The first three chapters describe some of the settings in which work with maladjusted children is carried on. The places described do not attempt to simulate family life but contain groups of boys or girls of similar age and attainment. The next two articles are both concerned with the importance to a child of his links with his own parents and family, each of the articles emphasizing a different approach to this subject, a contrast arising from differences in the degree of disturbances in the children and the purposes of the two settings described. The articles by Mrs Dockar-Drysdale and Mrs Winnicott carry us into the fantasy world which disturbed children inhabit and describe ways in which adults can communicate and make special individual relationships with a child through entering into his fantasy and allowing it to have acceptable symbolic expression.

Residential workers who for long periods have to relate on a feeling level to the unreal or to the primitive in children may find themselves being emotionally overwhelmed or depleted. The final two articles describe ways in which staff can be supported and sustained by group therapeutic techniques or consultation. These occasions provide opportunities for staff to recognize that their vulnerable points as well as their strengths can be used as a means of deepening their understanding of children's underlying feelings and also of furthering the formation of healing relationships with them. The residential treatment of disturbed children certainly makes heavy personal demands on adults. Residential workers can, however, take heart from Dr Anthony's reminder that there is a need to give and take in all human relationships and it is reasonable to enjoy receiving love as well as giving it.

ROBERT J. N. TOD

I

Therapeutic factors in group living

Child Welfare, vol. 35, January 1956.

Elliot Studt

The first article, by Mrs Studt, written in a condensed style, that repays careful attention, describes the aspects of living in a group that are therapeutic or healing to emotionally hurt children. She suggests that children whose capacity for relationships is underdeveloped or damaged are unable to respond to the demands of parent substitutes in Homes that try to reproduce family life. She outlines the following positive experiences that the therapeutic group can supply which the family setting cannot: the expectations of adults whether for emotional response or for conformity can be less; children with mixed-up feelings about parents may find it easier to adapt to a routine than to comply with the demands of a person; newcomers may receive support and comfort from other children who have previously encountered neglect or rejection; in a group setting, behaviour, which would have been disruptive of family life, can be seen as a symptom and so more easily be tolerated. In every case, however, the group must be on the watch against becoming remote or out of touch from normal life in the community.

Readers should bear in mind that the settings described by Mrs Studt are likely to contain groups of boys or of girls of a similar age rather than the so-called family groups of children of a wide age range to which we are accustomed in Britain. Perhaps Mrs Studt's ideas for 'fringe programmes' will be new to many; they are ways of planning for the child who cannot fit in.

This paper was originally given at the Child Welfare Section of the National Conference of Social Work in San Fransisco, California, U.S.A., in June 1955.

The processes by which each individual does his living—as differentiated from those involved in work, education, and play—

and the people with whom he shares his living, constitute a core experience which at any one time significantly influences his growth, productivity, mood, and general ability to make use of resources in other areas of functioning. Because living in a family is so psychologically and culturally imperative in our society we prefer to use the foster home, when substitute care is necessary for a child, since it provides the basic emotional experiences essential for development. Professional responsibility, we know, must be exercised in the selection of foster home and child for each other, and assistance must be provided to child, foster family, and own parents as they move through this not fully normal, and therefore sometimes problematical, set of relationships. When there is such professional help, foster home living can have significant corrective effects on a child's distorted attitudes and expectations from life. However, the great contribution of the foster home lies in the deep, sub-aware patterning of a child's emotional life through the day-to-day family living with all that this implies for mature personality development. This contribution of the foster home is most creative as it emerges spontaneously from the relationships that develop within the child-foster family constellation through repeated interactions of foster parents and child. Professional sense is needed to protect and support rather than to direct this grafting of the needy child into the life of the vigorous and independent social unit.

We make it too simple for ourselves if we try to think of living in a group as contributory to developmental processes in the same way that family living can be for the child who can use a foster home. Although we recognize the importance of group experiences in personality development we see them as part of a later developmental stage providing for the emotional reworking toward flexible social functioning of relationship patterns developed in the family rather than substituting for family experience. We are therefore rightfully concerned to understand what we do to a child's development when we set him within a situation in which for months at a time his living goes on in groups rather than in a family. Empirically we have found that some children use such group experiences far more constructively than they seem to be able to use family living. We have ceased to think unrealistically of group living as a thin substitute for family living in which cottage parents can be expected to provide for several children the same kind of care they would provide in their own homes for a foster child or two. We have come to recognize that certain characteristics of group living, apparently arising from the fact of groupness, are specifically useful for work with certain kinds of disturbed youngsters. But we have not yet clearly formulated what these characteristics are and how they can be combined to make the maximum therapeutic impact on the children under group care.

When we are working with a child whose ability to relate is so underdeveloped or damaged that he cannot at once use family living for growth, then we have to find some way of providing him with relationships which will help him begin to attach the business of living to positive personal experiences with human beings. It seems to me that group living is the setting within which we set about such a task. The factors of the group living situation which make this undertaking possible and which differentiate it from the foster home are those which provide greater control of the living process for therapeutic purposes. These are as follows:

1. The first of these factors is the presence in the group living unit of a houseparent—an adult or a series of adults who are employed to focus on the welfare of the children. This fact automatically reduces in the individual child expectations for giving love and provides a larger measure of child-focused energy for professional use.

A child going to the foster home must be able to give some satisfactions as well as to receive them. He must be capable of becoming in some measure a part of an ongoing cultural unit with purposes of its own over and above the professional purpose of meeting his needs. In fact, the foster home ceases to be a home unless the foster parents and siblings seek and receive from the new family member some contribution to their family life. The sharing by the foster child in such family life with its opportunity to give as well as to receive is one of the values which we covet for him and which requires a child of sufficient personal development to be able to enter, at least in minimal fashion, into sharing of this kind.

Although we hope that the child in the institution will be able to experience many aspects of this sharing, the fact that the adult in the group living unit is employed and has a base for personal living outside the child's world reduces in large measure the structural demand on the child. The adult is employed to serve the child's needs within his hours of employment. He is expected to seek his personal satisfactions outside these hours. It is therefore possible to expect of the houseparent in the group living unit more professionally focussed giving and less demand for receiving from the child than is possible in foster family living. This is an especially important dynamic to consider in planning for the child who is so deeply damaged that he will require long periods of care before he can enter into any sort of consistent relationship which involves both giving and receiving. The fact of employment of the responsible adult in the group living situation also provides for much more professional influence over the adult's behaviour through in-service training, supervision, and consultation. Thus, in the group living situation, one starts with a structure in which specific portions of an adult's time and energy have been purchased for use in relation to therapeutic purposes. The houseparent is therefore under obligation for a functioning of a more professional sort than is possible or desirable in a foster home.

2. The second factor is the presence of a group of peers. This factor can be used both to enhance certain satisfactions and to decrease certain tensions for those children who are not yet ready for the more intimate one-to-one relationships of the foster home. For instance, certain enjoyments are more intensely experienced by children of school age when others are present with whom it is easy to identify. Certain humorous situations are much more delightful when shared with others of the same developmental period; certain games which can be woven in and out of living routines are fun chiefly because they are shared with others of equal ebullience. By the same token there can be a significant reduction in tensions because of the presence of peers. It is the exceptionally disturbed child who can feel with equal intensity the sense of rejection at the hands of society when he is sharing group living with others of his own age who have gone through similar difficulties resulting in institutional placement.

4

In group living there tends to be an important depersonalization of rules and procedures because they apply to every one alike. The sense of a structure which applies to all can reduce the intensity of the adult-child confrontation over issues involving conformity. And such rules, properly designed, can appeal to and mobilize support from the group codes which appear among the children in achieving the behaviour necessary to comfortable group life. Thus the experience of necessary social controls may seem less oppressive to the individual child and less focussed in a battle with particular adults. The experience of living with a group of peers can thus be relied upon to magnify certain gratifications in the living experience, and to reduce through depersonalization and diffusion the tension-producing impact of certain necessary expectations and controls.

3. The third factor grows out of the second factor but needs to be mentioned for its specific contribution. This is the routinized structure or schedule clearly required whenever a number of equals live together.

In a foster home each individual is at a different level of development and function and so tends to have a schedule developed in relation to his individual needs. To adults and to children alike it seems obviously necessary to have a more precise structure for living when a group of peers live together. Thus even the very rebellious child accepts more easily that bathroom behaviour, for instance in relation to brushing teeth at bedtime, requires more routinization when several children with the same going-to-bed hour use the bathroom, than is necessary in a family where each child has his own bedtime based on age and school programme. This structure which is basic for all in the group tends to give security to control-hungry children. It can be built into a way of doing things which gives comforting support through the external structure to the child who is the victim of his own impulses. Its impersonal momentum reduces the demand on him for decision and self-control at crucial moments when his own control system is weak or reduced in efficiency. This schedule is not in itself a tool of inner change but it can provide the benign external fabric which subtly supports and directs the child toward satisfactions achieved through acceptable behaviour and away from behaviour which exhausts him and his environment. Within this structure more energy can be released for growth and through gradual and repeated experience with an ordered way of life techniques for self-direction may be learned.

4. A fourth important factor is the relative freedom to vary the design of the living experience according to the needs of the particular group of children.

In a foster home the style of living must be determined to a large extent by cultural influences unrelated to the needs of the foster child. The primary therapeutic decision, in foster home care, is made at the time of the selection of the particular child for the home rather than in determining a design for living after the child is placed. In the group living situation, however, ways of living can be established for therapeutic purposes which would be quite unacceptable for normal family life. Group living may take on forms as needed by the individuals in the group whether or not these forms are culturally acceptable as normal living patterns, and can vary both with the particular group and with the stages through which the group develops.

Since these factors are present in all group living, the possibility of their being barriers to treatment unless they are used with professional awareness for treatment purposes is present in all institutional care. We have all observed the inaccessibility to treatment of those children who are under the care of obtuse or punitive cottage parents; the barriers to communication set up by the informal peer group structure in the institution where group formation is left to itself; the deadening effect of routines; and the ease with which the institutional community becomes remote from and unrelated to the normal community culture. These are potent factors which, left to themselves in the artificial and self-enclosed community that is the institution, proliferate all the evils of rigidity and sterility which we tend to ascribe to institutional living. They are, in fact, dangerous factors unless used consciously for professional purposes. When, however, they are seen to be dynamic processes which can be organized into a therapeutic design for treatment purposes, the designing of group living in the institution becomes one of the most challenging of professional tasks. Given group living which has been designed in relation to the needs of a given group of children through the imaginative use of all these factors, several special aids to treatment become available.

Perhaps the primary contribution of the well-designed group living process is the way it provides for all sorts of individualization. Usually in approaching group living from the vantage point of group work, we have considered that the child's experiences in the group are the primary contribution of group living to his development. I find, however, when I think of my own institutional work with children, that I gave first place, in evaluating the special contribution of group living to treatment, to the base which the group life provides for individualized programmes for children on the fringe of the group. Such fringe programmes may be either temporary, providing protection for the child who is normally part of the group, or more extended programmes by which the seriously deviant child is kept close to the group although not part of it. It was our experience, even in a detention institution where the group was continually changing, where children were in crisis and were rarely long with us, that a vigorous and continuing group life could be achieved which satisfied the needs of most of the children most of the time and which was strong enough to allow for the flexible provision of all sorts of individualized programmes on the fringe of the central core of activity.

It was nine-year-old Rudy who taught us about fringe programmes. He was brought to us in a state of rage, grimacing and gnashing his teeth. The probation officer's report at intake said he lived with seven adults none of whom could run fast enough to catch him, that he never sat down to a meal with others, and that he was in the first grade at school because when he was in school he spent all of his time in annoying antics. His first day with us he spent tearing his clothes, urinating on the floor, breaking windows and screaming that he was being beaten. Wherever he went he climbed, or walked on his hands, in preference to using his feet.

We found out how to live with Rudy by setting up a plan for fifteen-minute shifts in programme which moved him from big muscle activity into quiet pursuits and back again and used every adult in the institution at different periods in his schedule.

At first this programme went on parallel to the group programme but gradually Rudy began to be able to tolerate eating with the group, and could join game hour when he had the attention of a counsellor to himself at a side table. As he relaxed still further, periods of play with another child could be planned. Because all the children accepted the fact that various kinds of individualization might be provided for any of them according to their needs, Rudy attracted little attention from the others and the group process proceeded as usual. It was of utmost importance that the group process was available for use as little by little Rudy began to be able to share in portions of it.

The group was saved the destructive experiences which would have resulted if he had entered into full membership from the first, yet neither was Rudy isolated entirely, and even in his most remote periods he could feel himself part of a larger community which included both his programme and the programme in which the other children were involved.

Thus, the well designed group living experience offers an exceptionally flexible base for each child's movement in and out of group experience. More easily than in a family, the individual in the group living process may move into a position of relative isolation; while at those points where he is able to bear group experience, easy and unobtrusive return to the group will be possible. Because of the more flexible and viable relationship between the individual and the group than is possible between child and family there also tends to be a greater range of tolerance of behaviour than can be permitted in the smaller, more compact, family unit. This wide flexibility of group life provides for individual patterns of living within the total design, for spontaneous group experiences when the child is able to relate with others, and for a freer individual expression of symptoms with less damage to others.

A second important therapeutic tool of the well designed group living situation relates to group experience as such. The variety of adults and the number of different children provide the individual with a wide variety of ways of relating within the group. Thus the child who is too fearful to bear real closeness to family substitutes is allowed to practice with human beings of many sorts for short or long periods of time as he can bear the contact. Although this diffuseness of relationship is a hazard for the child who has become able to achieve closeness, it is a benign factor for the fearful child which allows him to return again and again to those relationships which are rewarding and to remain more remote from those which are disturbing. Because of this multiplicity of relationship resources in the group, as the child grows he can experiment, according to the content of the living activities, with many roles in the group and with a variety of sub-group patterns. Where the adult leadership is skilled and the group is sufficiently mature he may be helped to move, within the accustomed patterns of daily living, into advanced group experiences in leadership and followership roles.

A third important tool found in therapeutically designed group living grows out of the combination of the group experience with the content of daily living. This combination gives group experience a peculiarly rich symbolic, sub-verbal content which can be used as an extra emotional valence to give group experiences as they happen especially significant impact. Because group living is concerned with the basic aspects of biological and hence of emotional life, with eating, sleeping, toileting, cleanliness, and the giving and receiving of affection, what happens in the group may reach through to feelings more directly and meaningfully than in any of the more formal group experiences where the content is concerned with education and recreation. Thus the individual who has not had in his own family the positive experiences with processes of living which are necessary for normal development, may find in the group a new way through to relationships in sharing such basic experience. Both his orientation to the activities and his ability to relate to other human beings may be enriched because of this conjunction of group experience and living processes with its potentiality for spontaneous sharing of emotions with other human beings. Because this kind of sub-verbal life material is the content of group living there should probably not be automatic transfer of group work methods [i.e. methods used in recreational groups] drawn from more traditional settings into the group living situation. It may well be that the group living group, given its repeated reassembling during the day and given the activities which provide its content, may require particular pattern and techniques differing in many ways from what is appropriate to other kinds of group work activities.

Although we have mentioned only three of the important tools for treatment which become uniquely available when the dynamic factors available in group living are properly organized for therapeutic purposes, other tools appear as the group living process develops with appropriate responsiveness to the needs of any particular group. As yet, experimentation in the use of group living as the basic treatment tool of the institution has only begun. However, we can suggest some of the principles with which it is necessary to be concerned when undertaking to organize the factors of group living into a therapeutic design. Four areas require particular attention in undertaking such a project. These are:

1. Special care must be given to the selection of individual children for group life, with particular effort to avoid imposing group living on children who are capable of the more emotionally advanced and culturally rich life of the family.

In other words we must not use group living for those children for whom such manner of living is a deprivation of emotional experiences for which they are ready. Rather it must be used as a specifically chosen tool for children who require that the living process be therapeutically controlled in the treatment of their difficulties.

2. We must learn much more than we now know about how to group children for group living.

Fritz Redl has suggested some of the factors to which we must give attention if we are to plan group living for maximum value to the individual children in our care. For instance he has found that there must not be too great a range within the group among developmental stages, between extremes of cultural taste, and in types of personality organization for impulse control. At the same time the group should provide certain important kinds of variety among the children. Experimentation and theory development is required in this area before we can with confidence plan assignment of individuals to group living groups.

3. The group living group must be carefully related to other groups and activities in the institution if it is to provide the full measure of its potential contribution.

For instance it must not be allowed to drop into the institutional blind spot as though it were simply a facilitating provision which keeps the children available for participation in other programme and treatment resources. Neither should it be made responsible for functions which should be provided through other groups such as recreation and community participation. The group living function must be specifically understood and provided for in the institutional plan, and the living group must be given status, facilities, and professional supervision in order to maximize its particular contribution. Group living is the central tool of institutional treatment and as such must be given its rightful place in an institutional programme.

4. It is particularly important to make the adults who are responsible for the group living process equal, respected and contributing members of the institutional staff.

If the group living group is to make its appropriate treatment contribution within the institutional programme, the personnel responsible for this function must have sound participation in the treatment team.

From an increasing number of reports from institutions who undertake to develop therapeutically designed group living programmes for their children, we will learn more about principles of work with the living group and will become able to think more precisely and professionally about institutional care for those children in need of such service.

Mrs Elliot Studt first studied English before the war at the University of California and later gained a Master's degree in Social Work, specializing in child welfare, at the University of Denver, and in 1957 a doctorate in social work at the University of Columbia, on this occasion making a special study of the care of children in detention. She has been Assistant Superintendent of a Detention Home, a caseworker and supervisor of social work students and has also been a Professor at the School of Social Welfare at the University of California. She is at present a research worker at the Centre for the Study of Law and Society at the University of California and lectures in the School of Social Welfare there. She has published a number of articles on casework in the correctional field, on delinquency, and on social work education for staff in institutions for delinquents.

2
Human relations in the institutional treatment of maladjusted and delinquent children

The Howard Journal, vol. 9, no. 2, 1955.

Marjorie Franklin

Throughout Dr Franklin's paper we are made aware of her warmth, concern and human feeling for disturbed and unhappy children. She believes that the residential hostel or school can be used to supplement child guidance treatment and stresses that the essential contribution of such settings is the attitude of the child-caring staff to children; an attitude which should comprise respect, friendliness, tolerance, informality, sincerity and ability to accept manifestations of feeling. Does she underestimate the difficulties of maintaining such an attitude in the face of hostility and indifference? In a later article Dr Anthony reminds us of the negative feelings that staff inevitably feel when living with difficult children and discusses how such feelings can be recognized and faced.

In former times, if a child was found to be suffering physically or mentally within an unsatisfactory family setting, and especially if in consequence he had become a behaviour problem, the indication was believed to be to remove him from a home with a small 'h' to a 'Home' with a capital 'H', the accent being on the removal rather than on the nature of the place to which he was taken. The more modern and better way is to accept the strong ties of family 'belongingness' and to treat both the home and the child in relation to each other, through the facilities of a child guidance or similar unit, providing, among other methods of rehabilitation, out-patient treatment.

For some maladjusted children of adolescent or pre-adolescent age a period of environmental in-patient treatment is desirable in the course of family adjustment or as an adjunct to it. In particular it is of value for selected children who have responded favourably up to a point from out-patient psychotherapy and have thereby developed some capacity to form relationships, but in whom progress has come to a standstill. A special environment, even without concomitant individual psychotherapy, can often enable such children, and sometimes even children who have been unresponsive to previous therapy, to make sufficient adjustment to be able eventually to cope with the strain of normal life or even with the disharmonies and inadequacies which their own homes offer.

To meet this need there have arisen hostels, hostel-schools and special boarding schools for maladjusted children–the distinction between the first and the two last being whether the institution provides teaching or whether the children go out to local schools.

The methods used in these hostels and schools vary one from another, both in broad principles which are matters of conscious decision and in subtler and more intangible ways which depend on personality and the impact of one individual on another. Selecting a child for a particular hostel or school, and preparing the child for going there are matters requiring skilled diagnosis and a knowledge of the places available. The choice depends partly on definite criteria such as age, sex, intelligence, type of maladjustment–partly on criteria which vary from time to time with the category of children present.

Maladjustment now forms a specific category of handicapped children and is recognized by the Ministry of Education. It comprises various kinds of psychoneurosis and various kinds of disturbances in character development, including incipient psychopathic personalities. I do not know of any reliable computation of the proportion of juvenile maladjusteds who steal, commit acts of violence, play truant or are beyond the control of parents or guardians; nor do I know the proportion of child offenders who suffer from some form of maladjustment. In both it is undoubtedly high. It is certain, however, that if all maladjustment in children were cured and all new cases prevented from occurring, we should have helped some children who would never have become delinquent, and also that juvenile offenders would still exist. Nevertheless, I believe that we should have broken the back of the problem of juvenile delinquency and that those who remained would be mainly the less intractable.

Love, warmth of feeling, reasonable freedom, and keen interests are needed by all children, including the maladjusted. However, it does not suffice for cure merely to provide an environment that might have prevented the disturbances arising. The schools and hostels under discussion aim at remedying maladjustments that have already occurred and thus the pattern is not necessarily and in detail the same as that of a good school and home for normal children – there are old hurts to assuage and new adjustments to be made which are different and additional to the gradual expansion involved in normal growing up.

A psychiatrist should be, and I think usually is, available to all institutions for maladjusted children, at the very least in a diagnostic and advisory capacity. In some hostels or schools selected children (seldom every child in the institution) receive, in addition to the therapeutic atmosphere of their daily life which is available to all, special treatment at regular times, such as interviews with a psychiatrist or play therapist, tuition from an educational psychologist, and so on. These periods, although often important and desirable adjuncts, are interpolated into the daily living. It is with this daily living that we are chiefly concerned here. It should be designed to promote conditions in which good relationships are formed, impulses and feelings can be expressed, guided or controlled, interests and talents cultivated and a better understanding gradually acquired of the art of living with others in harmony and mutual benefit, though without uniformity or standardization, for these children tend to be individualists.

Much of the success of environmental therapy depends upon the principles and methods used, and these to some extent can be taught, and should not be haphazard but should form a coherent pattern. Much, also, depends on the people in charge, and the demands on these are very great. Therapists and teachers engaged in non-residential work see patients or pupils for a specific period of time only, during which they are therapists or teachers and little else: they have not to administer their households, write letters or meet friends while the children are present, or at least while they are accessible to them. This is required of those who live at the same time as ordinary human beings and as parent respresentatives and as parent auxiliaries, for many of the children at hostels and schools for maladjusted children possess functioning parents. To these parents they will eventually return, and probably do return during holidays, and the parents should visit the child in the school or hostel environment. This lays the seed of healthier home relationships. It is the task of resident staff to live among a crowd of emotionally disturbed children without themselves becoming upset either in reaction to the children or to each other. It is, furthermore, their task to try to help these children to become less emotionally disturbed and at the same time to feed them, attend to their clothing, house them and see that they acquire knowledge. Teachers while paying regard to the symptoms of maladjustment and realizing that emotion often interferes with learning and that disturbed minds may be helped by interest, must also pay adequate regard to the obligation to teach those who are in a condition to imbibe knowledge. Food is a token of love and symbolically meaningful. It must also nourish. Clothes must be washed, mended, renewed, must be serviceable for warmth, hard wear and self respect, and so on, and also express personal predilections and idiosyncracies. The use of clothes for self expression is obvious to an observant visitor to a reasonably informal school, where may be seen such distinctive articles of apparel as weird headgear, cowboy belts, sweaters copied from those of an admired staff member, etc. Younger children have their bathing and going to bed supervised, and perhaps are regaled and tranquillized by a bed-time story. Those who attend to these matters and also to such duties as bedmaking, sewing or dusting, and are thus approximating to the activities of the children's mothers, and who can be naturally and informally accessible to children while working, are in a favourable position to observe emotional behaviour and to exert influence. This may be more difficult for a teacher who is engaged in specific and concentrated work. The former, therefore, should as far as possible be persons of education and members of the therapeutic staff. Adequate leisure for study, for meeting people and for relaxation is important for all workers in this field, especially senior staff, and they should not be exhausted by physically arduous chores. Nevertheless, in general, however unorthodox this may seem, it is an advantage if the Warden and

Matron of a Hostel School (who are the most influential people therapeutically) are personally concerned in some domestic, home-making occupations, the value of which to the community is obvious, which have parental associations, in which the children can give voluntary help and yet to which the adults need not give, while working, their entire attention, and thus can keep their minds free to consider as well the changing moods and demands of individual children.

The resident staff, then, have to cope with hourly demands and daily crises, accept love and hate from the children and give understanding friendliness and affection. They must recognize and endure the trials of being the objects of 'testing out' experiments, and expect the symptoms of maladjustment to be manifested. They are not there only to 'manage', tactfully, difficult children. They must do this, but they should also and chiefly try to engender a state of easement of anxieties and of conflicts to the point where spontaneous living, without the need for being specially 'managed' and without being restrained through fear of consequences, is conducted in a way that is both socially acceptable and personally satisfying. An environment, so organized that the children always appear serene and are consistently well behaved and productively occupied, is less likely to achieve permanent success than one where some of the symptoms of not yet cured maladjustment can be manifested. The adults in such an environment should be alive to those occasions where it is wise to be satisfied with, indeed rather to welcome, an exhibition of behaviour and of imaginative play appropriate to a stage of childhood earlier than that of either the child's chronological or mental age; and should also know when to encourage responsibility and more mature interests. Staff should at times identify with the child and be able to enter into his world, in so far as an adult can, and yet always be ready to exert adult control when needed. They must be able to give the child a feeling of security and confidence even during his unbridled moments, and to do so without his feeling that he is being nagged and perpetually under criticism. All this requires judgment, sensitivity, balanced tolerance and enough nervous stability and detachment for the job. These are not vague generalizations, but necessities for first-class work in the healing care of maladjusted children through environment and relationship.

As already mentioned, there are many types of good institutions for the residential treatment of maladjusted children (as well as some that are not so good). In some the accent and focus for cure is the individual treatment they receive from psychotherapists, who may be members of the staff or otherwise, in intimate contact. In the larger number, whether or not some individual psychotherapy is given, the main accent is on the methods of handling and educating used by the staff and on community living although, as already mentioned, visiting psychiatrists should be attached to these also. The majority of schools and hostels, then, depend mainly on social therapy combined with general advice and discussions with staff from visiting specialists, who may give individual children occasional interviews. Some institutions make use of child guidance clinics, to which selected children are sent out, instead of a psychiatrist seeing them in the institution. Where the standard of values in the institution is mainly behaviouristic, a separation of psycho-therapy, with its emphasis on causation and unconscious mental functioning and interpretation, may not be a disadvantage. When, however, the methods of the institution are constructive, it is mutually helpful if both forms of approach can be combined in a way that is only possible within the community. Children who go to places where environmental therapy is the chief factor benefit from a period of non-residential psychotherapy before admission. In some cases it may be desirable after leaving.

Maladjusted children in general are deficient in the power to form object relationships and in their sense of reality. Institutions depending largely on community treatment need, if they are to succeed, to provide sufficient control to allay anxiety in a nervous child and also to prevent an aggressive child disrupting the place and the neighbourhood. There must be sufficient protected freedom for self expression, release of feelings, and also for the acting out of preconscious phantasies in play and in creative work, individually and in association; also opportunities for establishing new relationships. In many cases behaviour involving a return to an earlier developmental stage necessarily precedes real improvement, but opportunities should be given also for establishing sublimations and exercising responsibility. In educating disturbed children and adolescents use may be made of spontaneous imaginative

games and activities to which adults contribute neither suggestions nor intervention. Psychological interpretations should
be avoided unless given by people qualified to do so. Organized
games also have their place and there is great value in aesthetic and
creative outlets through music, painting, dance, drama and literature, woodwork and various crafts. It is, in my experience, invalu-
able as a means of helping to direct the thinking habits and actions
of anti-social children towards social betterment for them to participate in community government. Some experienced workers find
great help in co-education.

These are only a few among many internal tasks which must be
tackled within a good hostel or school. I would like also to stress
the very great importance of promoting better relations between
the children and their parents, or the people with whom they make
their homes, implying regard and consideration on both sides.
This problem may be dealt with partly by children spending part
of school holidays at their homes, the visits being long enough to
give a reality relationship and to supplant the imaginary parents
who become vivid phantoms in the minds of children prevented
from seeing them in the flesh. But the visits should not be long
enough (except as a trial period before leaving) for old problems
and troubles to become acute, or to necessitate fresh adaptation to
the school on return. The bettering of relationships with the
family is also tackled by encouraging parents to visit their
children informally at the school, where they can discuss their
own child with those in charge and see him among a group of
others. In this way they may learn to view him in a new light. The
problem of home adjustment is also tackled at a distance with the
co-operation of social workers. Moreover, a temporary absence of
a disturbed and disturbing child gives an opportunity for establishing harmony in a home.

Though one could put forward some general ideas based on
theory and experience, it is not yet possible to say with assurance
when a child can be adequately helped only by deep individual
therapy and when the more diffuse but more superficial, global
methods are to be preferred. It has already been noted that the
total period of treatment is likely to be shorter if a child has some
psychotherapeutic treatment before admission. Some individual
treatment after leaving would probably in many cases help to

stabilize improvement, but in practice such advice is seldom followed if symptoms and character have improved.

In summarizing the methods available for environmental therapy, special prominence should be given to the attitude of staff to children, the impact of which is often a new experience to a child. This attitude should comprise respect, friendliness, tolerance, informality, sincerity and ability to accept manifestations of feeling. Important in its influence on rehabilitation is a régime in which control of conduct is not based on rewards and punishments. Among constructive activities, I have seen benefit ensue from children sharing with adults in the actual erection and furnishing of the primitive buildings in which this community lived. There should be opportunities for, and encouragement of, artistic and cultural interests. Maladjusted children enjoy, perhaps to an older age than do untroubled children, outlets in unorganized play, as, for example, in constructing wigwams and their own rough-hewn camps. They need the kind of activities which express phantasies and which give constructive and destructive outlets. Some form of community government seems to me essential for young people over about eleven with whom social therapy is undertaken. Its form and details differ widely at different places where it is used, and at one place at different times. Ventilation of grievances and also of constructive ideas in words, the open and objective discussion of instances of misbehaviour, and suggestions for preventing recurrences, the propounding of simple laws for the better arrangement of daily living, and, in particular, engagement in practical discussions directed beyond the self to wider questions of advantage to the community as a whole, or to particular sections of it—all this is no less valuable than executive power. This executive power should not be in the hands of individual children but of the group of adults and children together. It should be great enough to give a sense of participation, achievement and responsibility and a realization that inconvenience follows unwise decisions, but the power should not include matters whose mismanagement might disrupt the community or involve serious anxiety or interfere with the health or welfare of anyone. An onlooker or observant adult participant at these community meetings can gain an insight into the more healthy and mature side of these children and their often surprising good sense;

such insight may prevent over-emphasis on the immaturity that is also characteristic of maladjusted persons.

Improvement may be due to the factors mentioned and to others, but we have much to learn regarding the dynamics of the changes. It is a theme worthy of further study. I suggest that the components of change include: relief of tension and of anxiety; relief of primitive guilt feelings; increase in a sense of personal dignity and value. A sense of safety and security is helped by the attitude of the adults and by community government. The opportunity for temporary regression, which is really a relaxation of spurious maturity, is important. I have referred a good deal to expressing and acting out phantasies, giving controlled outlets for impulses and aptitudes, and have also stressed the importance of sublimation. The formation of good object relationships is essential to good social adjustment. As aggression diminishes there evolves a greater power to mix with others. In some cases it seems that there are changes also at the instinctive level and that the deeper layers of the mind may be affected in a rather complicated way.

In reasonably successful use of planned environmental therapy we are entitled to expect transference and identification to be stages leading to an ability to form genuine attachments. It should lead also to a more highly developed ego, a more mature super-ego, a greater tolerance of reality with its inevitable frustrations, and a greater willingness to serve the community. Besides helping to overcome weaknesses due to maladjustment, the education should aim to build on and develop such healthy assets of the personality as are unaffected by the maladjustment, and thus by-pass the symptoms.

Finally, if it gives nothing else, it is essential that the school or hostel provide a period in the children's lives when they experience care-free, childish happiness. If it gives that, the sojourn will mean something of value in after life, even if the after history is not in every respect all that is to be desired.

Marjorie Franklin received her medical and psychiatric training in London, Baltimore and Boston and trained as a psycho-analyst under Dr Sandor Ferenczi in Budapest. She has been consultant psychiatrist at the Portman Clinic sponsored by the Institute for the Study and Treatment of

Delinquency and was co-founder of Q camp for delinquent and maladjusted men and a second camp for boys with similar problems. She was a founder and co-psychiatrist at Alresford Place residential hostel school for maladjusted boys and girls and served for ten years on the Committee of the Association of Workers for Maladjusted Children.

3
The natural history of detention

Case Conference, vol. 11, no. 7, January 1965.

Frank Bodman

In this article Dr Bodman describes to us the behaviour and feelings of older boys who come to an approved school by order of a juvenile court and not of their own choice. He tells us about four stages of reaction to separation and placement through which boys pass. The mourning for loss of liberty and loss of family life is also mentioned by Mr Moss in the article that follows.

The article is based on a lecture given at Ruskin College, Oxford, in 1964.

There is a natural history of imprisonment, which results in certain responses and adaptations, whether the 'prison' is a boarding school, an approved school, a borstal, a prison or a concentration camp.

We may congratulate ourselves that conditions in approved schools have been progressively becoming more liberal in the last two decades, with longer and more frequent home leaves, encouragement and subsidization by travel vouchers of parental visits, privilege leaves, weekend hikes, and camping expeditions; but it remains a fact that from the boy's point of view, he sees at first the approved school order as a prison sentence, and reacts in his feelings accordingly.

What is the sequence in this natural history of detention? I think we can learn most by studying the extreme examples, realizing that in the average case we shall recognize some features only dimly illuminated rather than highlighted.

Elie Cohen[1] has made a study of human behaviour in a concen-

[1] Elie A. Cohen, *Human behaviour in the concentration camp*, Cape, 1954.

tration camp, himself a survivor, and in a book published by Jonathan Cape had devoted a chapter to the 'Psychology of the concentration camp prisoner'. He describes a stage of Initial Reaction, a stage of Adaptation, a stage of Regression, and a stage of Resignation.

I have seen all these stages in approved school boys, if only in miniature.

To describe these stages in more detail:

First, the *Initial Reaction*. This depends on what the boy thought would happen to him. He will have heard some gossip, some tall tales in the Remand Home, or if he comes from a delinquent area, heard the boasts of approved school boys on leave. He is often given some advice and information from his Probation Officer, but it is one thing to have some second-hand information, quite another to be faced with the inevitability of the reality.

One of the reactions in this initial stage is acute depersonalization. 'I felt as if I did not belong'–'As if the business did not concern me'. 'I felt no sympathy for the other new boys'. This depersonalization, or loss of identity, was made all the easier by the adoption of school uniform, the haircut, and the loss of identifying marks, rather like drakes going into a moult; no longer the Beatles hair cut, the pointed foot gear, the Italian shirt. In spite of the conception of approved school life previously formed, the reality was too painful for the ego to realize. The defence mechanism is a split into one who observes, and one to whom things happen.

The other reaction to be observed, though of course by no means so acute as in the concentration camp, is an acute fright reaction; this is more likely to happen to the boy who was not expecting an approved school order. He has had no period of anxious readiness to prepare for his new experience, but is suddenly faced with separation from home, as sometimes happens when the probation officer is instructed to take him straight to the approved school from the court house.

In such a reaction the boy will be 'jumpy' for days–there will be a decrease in the capacity to feel, shown by a loss of interest in his relatives, a lack of sympathy for mates in the same situation.

Or alternatively the boy may over compensate, develop aggressive reactions, refuse to be pushed around, will break the rules out of bravado, boast to staff and mates. In some cases this over compensation becomes quite pathological, the boy becomes hypomanic. We had one boy who said he was coming up to the Top Ten, had been interviewed at the B.B.C. and had an engagement to appear on television, and spent the night in the dormitory practising and rehearsing. Or the fright reaction may be followed by a stage of apathy; the boy shows no interest in his surroundings and is slow in all his reactions.

These initial reactions are not often seen in boys who have already experienced separation from home by being taken into care into children's homes or by being remanded for some weeks. Many boys nowadays have been in a Remand Home more than once before reaching the Classifying School, and the initial reactions of depersonalization, lack of feeling, euphoric bravado or apathy have been noted by the wardens of the Remand Home.

Usually this initial reaction does not last more than one or two weeks, and then follows a period of mourning, mourning for the loss of liberty, for the loss of family life, of the accustomed recreation of cafés or billiard halls and dances, of girl friends, of unlimited smoking. This miniature reactive depression may last for as long as six months, and tends to interfere with the stage of adaptation. There is a general lethargy, a loss of interest in work or play, a lack of ambition, a feeling of hopelessness that his situation could improve. But unlike the adult depressive states there is very rarely any self blame for the situation in which the boy finds himself.

In this state he can only look on the dark side of things, and in his letters home paints a gloomy picture of his life, the hard work, the bad food, the bullying, the boring chores, which is quite unjustified.

But usually at the end of the first term, and after the first home leave, the boy reaches the stage of adaptation.

He begins to accept the conditions of life in a closed community; the lack of liberty is balanced by the possibility of privilege leave at week ends, by the hope of home leave in three months. He still does not know how long he will have to spend in the approved school–the sentence is indeterminate, he cannot make realistic plans for the future, he rarely envisages a prospect beyond the return home.

He also learns to accept the restricted communications, the censorship of letters, the limited opportunities of speaking with outsiders.

For some boys, particularly the introverts rather than the extroverts, one of the greatest deprivations which is felt as punishment is the lack of privacy; the forced community life with boys of widely divergent temperaments and backgrounds. This is one of the factors that leads to irritability, to quarrels and fights. Some of these boys will be missing for some hours at a time. They do not abscond but disappear into the shrubberies or outhouses by themselves in a quest for what they call 'peace and quiet'.

At Kingswood Training School we have partitioned off the old 40-bed dormitories into cubicles of 4-5 beds; but it is important to sort out the boys into congenial groups as far as possible.

In the self-pitying stage, I find boys are often disappointed at the lack of sympathy from boys who have been longer in the school. In spite of having been found guilty in the Juvenile Courts, or even after an appeal has failed at Quarter Sessions, it is not unusual for a boy to maintain a feeling of being innocent, of having to suffer all this misery; they regard themselves as martyrs, victims of forces beyond their control and superior to their judges, magistrates, and instructors.

In this stage of adaptation, the most successful adapters are those who have been most thoroughly trained already in the struggle for life. The boy tries to discover how to live as well as possible within the restrictions of the approved school. Groups aggregate from the same town or region. Each one demands comradeship, but not every boy is prepared to be friendly. The majority are unfriendly to new arrivals who have had longer liberty than they have had. Gradually approved school life becomes the real life, and life outside the school becomes strange; the boys often feel that their families, the outside world, has no idea of what life in the approved school is like.

And so as in any closed community, the main topic of conversation is the school itself; there is a small-minded tendency, a heightened irritability, an intolerance of contradiction, a restless suspicious mood, reminiscent of the so-called 'barbed wire sickness' noted in prisoner-of-war camps.

In a community there must be some organization. For the boy

who comes from a 'problem family' or a slum area, it is a new experience to live by the clock, to eat at set times, sitting down to a table, to wash several times a day, to bathe or take a shower, to wear working clothes, to change clothes at set times, to go to bed relatively early in the evening; but to the boy who comes from an orderly home, and has had experience of some flexibility as he grows older, there is a tendency to regress as the responsibility for arranging his time-table is removed, and this regression often invades all areas of his life, so that enuresis recurs, he becomes slack about cleanliness, his language coarsens, and he talks smut.

This is often blamed by the parents on his forced association with criminal types, but in my view, there is often an emotional regression to be considered as well.

Lastly, of course, adaptation can be too successful, go too far. We speak of the child becoming institutionalized, so that he is unable to re-adapt when the time comes for him to rejoin society.

Nowadays the tendency is to release boys on licence a good deal earlier, but when I started this work 15 years ago, a large proportion of boys in intermediate schools stayed in school very nearly the statutory three years.

Some of these boys became over adapted and identified themselves with authority figures. They demanded discipline and obedience from the younger, newer and smaller boys, shouted at them, beat them up, stole clothes and tobacco from their mates and showed contempt for the human qualities of pity, compassion, sympathy.

These boys become a menace, a travesty of discipline and authority.

I remember one of these boys well, who on licence joined the army, and a year later came back to show himself off in the uniform of a Military Policeman.

It is important to recognize these reactions and not attribute them to other causes, and also to recognize them as phases in a general process to which all boys committed are liable. Until I understood this I had made an incorrect diagnosis of depression in several boys at the classifying school, which was not supported by behaviour at training school.

Before attempting to resolve an approved school boy's neurosis, it is essential to recognize his reaction to confinement, and give him some insight to his behaviour and why he is feeling and acting as he does; otherwise a confused and muddled relationship between psychiatrist and boy results.

Frank Bodman M.D., D.P.M. is a consultant psychiatrist with thirty years' experience of psychiatric work in child guidance. During the war years he was deputy director of the Bristol Child Guidance Clinic and for the past twenty-five years has been director of the Somerset Child Guidance Service. He has also been for a period of twenty years consultant psychiatrist to the Kingswood Training and Classifying Schools.

4

How children feel about
being placed away from home

Children, vol. 13, no. 4, July-August 1966

Sidney Z. Moss

Many residential workers will know of children who seem unable to grasp the reasons for being away from their parents, and are resentful at being unable to return home. They fear to mention the subject but at the same time want to explore it further. In this article Mr Moss says it is vital that children should be helped to talk about their feelings at the time of separation and placement. Only if they can experience a period of mourning for the real or imagined loss of their parents can they move on later to make new relationships.

Most children in child-care institutions today have parents. In fact, they have been called 'orphans of the living'.[1] Thus, when a child is placed in an institution, he faces two difficult adjustments: mastery of the separation trauma; and adaptation to life in the institution. As a former institutional case-worker, I have had the opportunity to observe how some children and their parents can convert an experience of being torn apart into a process which has been described as 'moving apart through growth'.[2]

I have also observed how difficult this process becomes when children have not been well prepared in advance for the separation and placement, when they have not been encouraged from the beginning to express their true feelings about these two frighten-

---

[1] Joseph H. Reid, 'Action called for–recommendations' in *Children in need of parents*, ed. Henry S. Maas and Richard E. Engler, Jr., Columbia University Press, New York, 1959.

[2] Frederick H. Allen, 'Mother-child separation: process or event?' in *Emotional problems of early childhood*, ed. Gerald Caplan, Tavistock Publications, 1955.

ing experiences, and when their parents have not been helped to build and maintain a meaningful relationship with them during the entire period of placement. In this article, I will discuss the effect of repressed feelings on such children after they have been in institutional placement for many months or even years and the implications of this for an institutional casework service.

The children I worked with were in long-term placement in an institution for dependent and neglected children which had only recently begun to offer intensive casework services. Many of them had been separated from their parents through juvenile court action. Many had lived in families in which there was long-time parental discord, alcoholism, or mental illness, and most had been subjected to serious neglect or abuse. Others came from homes broken by parental desertion, separation, physical or mental disability, or death.

The two basic fears of a child are said to be of loss of parental love and of parental desertion. As English and Pearson have pointed out,[1] when children lose a parent, whether through death, desertion, or themselves being sent away from home, they go through a mourning experience similar to an adult's after the death of a loved one. But each child must work out his mourning process in his own way. This will be affected not only by the child's own personality, but also by his age, sex, cultural background, the quality of his relationship with the lost parent, and his previous experiences of loss. For example:

Maria, an older adolescent, deserted as a little girl by her parents whom she never saw again, still follows every rumour about their whereabouts, scours telephone books, sees her parents in many strangers' steps.

The loss of a father generally has a more significant meaning to a boy's development than to a girl's. Also, the loss of the mother has a different impact on a girl than on a boy. For a boy, a father represents a model of masculinity with which he can identify as he works out his feelings of assertiveness, competitiveness, and independence. Moreover, having a father who can be depended on

[1] O. Spurgeon English and Gerald H. J. Pearson, *Emotional problems of living*, Allen & Unwin, 1949, p. 98.

may help him develop the ability to accept authority in others when appropriate. Similarly, for a girl loss of her mother represents a loss of an identification model. Also, since children, whether boys or girls, grow with certainty of their mother's love, loss of a mother or loss of her love (which to a child may be the same thing) impairs children's potential to trust in others. The resultant fear of rejection may become internalized as a fear of closeness.

As Charnley[1] has pointed out, unless children can freely discuss their situation at a time of parental loss, they are led to repress feelings of guilt, shame, ambivalence, and confusion about themselves and their parents and to withdraw into defences of mistrust, fantasy, and denial. Since placement away from home means parental loss to a child, the child begins with a serious handicap. No matter how well prepared children are for the placement, separation from their parents is still a traumatic experience for them and evokes psychic defences against the pain. Littner has shown that these defences, if internalized, can impede the development of other relationships, encourage repetition of the past trauma, and inhibit growth.[2]

No matter how long children have repressed or avoided their feelings about separation, they need to become aware of them to grow not only as independent beings but also in relation to their parents. Children, however, have ambivalent reactions to the idea of discussing their feelings about past separation. On one hand, they thirst for more understanding of the past–particularly of how and why they came into placement. They want to fill in the unknown facts and feelings of their past to know more about themselves and what they want to become. On the other hand, they do not feel strong enough to bear the pain of exploring their feelings. Glickman[3] has observed that a child resists discussion of his feelings about separation because he is afraid to 'lose all chance to return to the family, a hope he clings to in fantasy or unconsciously'.

[1] Jean Charnley, *The art of child placement*, University of Minnesota Press, Minneapolis, 1955.

[2] Ner Littner, *Some traumatic effects of separation and placement*, Child Welfare League of America, New York, 1956.

[3] Esther Glickman, *Child placement through clinically oriented casework*, Columbia University Press, New York and London, 1957.

Often children who resist discussing their parents in the hope that they will change are those whose parents are most inconsistent and rejecting. These are the parents who talk about taking the child home but never make any plans, who promise to visit the child and do not, who rarely write to him, who forget his birthday, and who care little about the child and his needs. Such children suffer deeply since they are constantly confused about what to expect from their parents. But they cannot express their resentment because of their hope that the parents might magically change after all, or because of their fear that the parents might sever the tenuous connection they have. Such children may transfer their conflicting feelings about their parents to the institution itself. Although they wish to trust their parents to meet their emotional needs, they are not sure they can, and this ambivalence is repeatedly acted out in erratic behaviour in the institution.

A child may also hide his feelings about separation behind a pseudo-mature objectivity. Outwardly, he is like an adult; inwardly, he is the child torn with yearning for his unmet dependency needs to be met.

> Joan, a pre-adolescent in placement many years, believes intellectually that her mother, who recently married, has a right to live a life of her own; but at the same time she is terribly hurt, depressed, and confused by her mother's rejection and preference for a strange man over her.

Children also resist discussing their parents when they have no home to go to. This is often true when their parents are dead.

Children are very protective of their parents, ready to defend them against any criticism, direct or implied. Many feel so much a part of their parents that to reveal any negative feelings about them seems like an indictment of themselves. They often want to be like their parents regardless of the way the parents have treated them.

> Sybil, recalling her mother, who was sexually promiscuous and alcoholic up to her death, literally worships her mother, as if any criticism of her meant complete rejection.

Children search for every scrap of attention they ever received as proof of their parent's love. They cannot bear to let their parents be considered neglectful or their love so weak as to have permitted separation to occur. Children cling to their old ties, no matter how destructive the parent-child relationship, in the absence of certainty about the new relationships available to them.

Children's resistance to discussing their feelings about their parents is also strengthened by the fact that a mere mention of parents reminds them of the reality of their placement and of their sense of abandonment, which they must deny to avoid pain. Some children accordingly meet mention of their parents with an air of indifference.

Johnny, an adolescent, has been in placement many years. He cannot remember his previous life in his parents' home. His mother died when he was four and he only vaguely remembers her funeral. His father is still living but rarely visits him in the institution. Johnny has built a wall around himself. He has no interest in his father now or in connection with the future. A sullen, withdrawn boy, he bullies other children and tortures animals.

Jimmy, a ten-year-old child, was deserted by his father shortly after he was born. His mother placed him with a relative, whom he thought was his mother until she died. Then his mother immediately had him placed in an institution. Now Jimmy cannot remember his substitute mother. He has little feeling for his own mother except resentment that she placed him so quickly. He knows that his father is alive but prefers to consider him 'dead'. 'What's the difference, he does not see me.' Jimmy has made sexual advances to a child of pre-school age. He now shows suicidal tendencies.

Some children resist discussing their parents because they do not want to give them up as objects upon which to project their resentment of the world. They need to reject their parents until the parents make up for their pain. Such children develop a superficial, exploitative, and demanding attitude which is carried into all relationships.

Mae, an older adolescent, was placed for institutional care by a deserted 'father' who suspects she is not his, although he does not tell her this. Desperately wanting him to love her but unable to trust in his feelings toward her, which she senses as ambivalent, she denies any feeling of affection toward him. Playing on his sense of guilt, she demands money and expensive gifts whenever she sees him. He complies but with deepening resentment.

Some children resist discussing their feelings about their parents because no one has ever before been concerned about how they feel and they do not see why anyone should be concerned now. Others feel relieved in finding that the caseworker understands a little of what it means to be a child in placement but resent the fact that nobody discussed their feelings with them when they first came to the institution. Some express a feeling of futility, saying that discussions about their parents now can have little value except as painful reminders of the past and of the pointlessness of the future.

As Rose has pointed out,[1] many children having been neglected before the placement have had little opportunity to develop a capacity for creative adaptation under stress. Although the institution may offer such children the kind of security and consistent good care that are conducive to healthy growth, they need to discover the positives in the situation themselves before they can deal effectively with their pain. There is pain in their efforts to reconcile the fact of their placement with their parent's expression of concern for them; pain in finding their worst fears confirmed – that their parents did not love them enough to keep them – especially bitter if they have brothers and sisters who have been kept home; pain in not knowing if they will ever be back with their parents, who are often vague in regard to their intentions; and pain in feeling inadequate and helpless in an unpredictable world – a feeling expressed in the frequent question, 'What will happen next?'

Most institutionalized children seem to have little idea of how and why they came into placement or what is planned for their future. Many do not remember at all how they came, who brought them, and how they felt at the time. This may be due to their swift

[1] John A. Rose, 'A re-evaluation of the concept of separation for child welfare' in *Child Welfare*, December, 1962

acceptance for care, without appropriate preparation, explanation, or help in dealing with their pain. Their primary means of defence then was to repress all feeling.

Sometimes parents have been unaware of their own motivations and so unable to give the children adequate reasons for the placement. Some parents who in their childhood have themselves been placed away from home unconsciously earmark a child for placement out of a need to repeat their past in working out their own unresolved conflicts.

Joan, according to her mother, was born at the wrong time—when the mother was depleted physically and emotionally. When Joan's father died, her mother let the grandmother take care of her for a while and then placed her in the institution. The mother later remarried. Joan now twelve years old, longs in vain to return to her mother, who continues to reject her. The mother has created the same situation with her child that she, herself, experienced as a little girl. She, too, lost her father, was quickly placed, and longed desperately for years to return to her mother, who remarried but had no room for her.

Sometimes a deserted mother has taken her revenge on the child.

Jane, whose father left home shortly after her birth, was placed in the instution at an early age because she was a constant reminder to her mother of the father's desertion. At the time of placement the mother said she could not handle the child until her husband returned. Actually, she had never wanted the baby, whose birth she felt was the cause of her husband's desertion. Jane, now seven, yearns for her lost father, but does not want to be returned to her mother.

Unable to accept the fact that their parents wanted to get them out of the home, some children blame the placement worker. They accuse the worker of talking the parents into it or stealing them when their parents were out. A child may feel that his placement came about by accident, that if his mother had not needed to go to a hospital on a particular day the placement worker would not have come to get him.

A child may initially see the institution as providing protection. But as years pass without adequate planning for the child's future, the child tends to see the institution as a permanent provider and becomes increasingly dependent upon it. If he cannot plan for the unknown future or master the trauma of his separation, he drifts complacently in the present.

When the caseworker discusses the possibility of reunion, the children frequently express a desire to stay in placement. They are afraid to leave the security and dependability of the institution. This is especially true of children who have been in placement for a long time. They want to avoid the risk of a more independent life and the need to work out a relationship with their parents; but they rationalize their resistance to reunion and may say they want to remain where they are for several years longer so they can graduate from school with their friends or that they do not like the neighbourhood where their parents live.

Some children deny that there is anything to prevent them from returning to their parents. They seem unaware of their parents' rejection or inability to care for them at home and fantasy that when they want to go home all they need to do is to ask their parents to take them. Other children blandly shrug off any discussion of going home to avoid the possibility of further anxiety and rejection. In fact, some children, emotionally drained by a long placement, may no longer be able to show much feeling for their parents.

Some children are realistic when the subject of reunion with their parents comes up. They have little faith in their parents' capacity and stress the value of security and dependability in the institution. They realize that their father cannot hold down a job or that their mother is unable to provide clean clothes, regular meals, and an adequate home for them.

Underlying some of the children's strong feelings of dependency on the institution may be the failure of the institution to encourage the parents to be actively involved with the child while he is in placement. The child's awareness that his parents seem undervalued may reinforce his own sense of inadequacy and lead to increasing reliance on the institution as a substitute family, at the expense of a developing sense of autonomy.

Children who have had little opportunity to express their feelings about separation and have had little sense of their own participation in the decision for placement tend to be anomic, with a diffuse sense of identity and little capacity for relationship. Having little idea of the reason for their placement, they have little sense of direction and consequently feel helpless. They have no plans for the future and when the caseworker brings up the subject they may ask, 'Where were you when I needed you? It's too late now.'

Even if the caseworker and the child develop a specific plan for the future, the child is likely to react with confusion, indecisiveness, and failure to follow through. When it is made clear to him that he is expected to follow through with whatever plan he has chosen, he may regard the expectation as rejection and react with anger or stubborn refusal.

The present may have little meaning for an institutionalized child. Said one, with a shrug: 'What's a birthday? One day is just like another—like death?'

Time spent in placement with no distinct goals can be death-like. Only a succession of discreet moments without continuity and direction, it fails to provide the momentum for growth, and the child is unable to proceed toward self-fulfilment. Lawder has pointed our how a child long in placement may retain the same symptoms of distress that he showed at the beginning.[1] He cannot move beyond that point until he has been helped to understand the reason for and the goals of the placement.

A child who has only a vague sense of identity feels an aching loss and a desperate need for others to make up for what he does not have, or to support what he does have. Yet, filled with both rage and self-hate, he is not sure he can trust in any human relationships. His energy is dissipated in clinging to others in an insatiable dependency bond, which gradually eats away his capacity to be a person in his own right.

Such a loss of identity prevents a child from seeing himself as the key person in charge of his own fate. Struggling with loneliness, he develops few interests, sees things only in black and white, 'reacts to' rather than 'feels with' other people and tends to regard people as objects to fill immediate needs. Having little sense of autonomy, he thinks mainly in terms of what others want him to

[1] Elizabeth A. Lawder, 'Can long-time foster care be unfrozen?' in *Child Welfare*, April, 1961.

be; and having little sense of purpose he marks time and avoids full use of the institutional programme or staff relationships. Since growth is possible only when time is, to employ an expression of Thomas Mann, 'sanctified by its creative use', such a child needs help in developing a sense of control over his time or destiny so that he can use the placement experience creatively.

Thus, in working with institutionalized children, it is essential to deal with their feelings about separation from their parents as early as possible before they are blocked by repression. Ideally, casework treatment with this focus should begin well before placement, or, if this is impossible, immediately afterward and should be carried on as long as the child is in placement, for pain and psychic conflict inflicted by parental loss are deep and tenacious. However, even when a child has been in placement a long time without having a chance to discuss his feelings freely, a sensitive caseworker may help him do so.

While the institution's caseworker may also help the child accept his parent's decision to place him away from home, the placement agency should impress upon the parent the importance of giving the child the initial explanation so that he may gain strength from the feeling that behind the decision was concern for himself. Similarly, the agency should make it clear to the parents that they are expected to keep in close touch with their child during the whole time he is in placement so that he can feel strong in his identification with his family, the source of so much of his individuality.

The agency's goals in accepting each child for placement also should be made clear to his parents, or parent, at the beginning of placement so that they will understand the importance of their full and continuous involvement in support of the agency's plan for the child. A clear understanding of what is expected of them can help motivate parents to maintain a positive connection with their children through responsible visiting, letter writing, backing plans to meet his medical needs, and working with the staff on his behalf. When parents are so involved, the children can learn to see the parents as they are and to value their strength and respect their limitations. This helps them make better use of the placement experience.

An institution must develop understanding of what it can expect from parents. Some parents may not be able to support a placement plan; some may be able to relate to their children in placement but may be against reunion; others may be realistically hopeful of having their children at home once more; still others may need help to relinquish their child so that he can be free for adoption or a foster-home placement.

If it becomes evident that a child may need to stay in long-term institutional care, this should be made clear to both parent and child, but the plan should be reviewed periodically.

Whether parent and child can be reunited or need to stay apart, the growth of each separately and in relation to each other is the placement goal.

Sidney Z. Moss is a graduate of the University of Pennsylvania School of Social Work and has worked in a number of children's agencies in Philadelphia including the Society to Protect Children and the Philadelphia Child Guidance Clinic. He is now chief psychiatric social worker at the Children's and Adolescent's Psychiatric Clinic, Philadelphia General Hospital.

5
Therapeutic use of visiting in residential treatment

Child Welfare, vol. 44, no. 5, May 1965.

Sylvester Adessa and
Audrey Laatsch

In the previous article the author mentioned the importance to a child of a continued link after placement with his own family, the source of so much of his individuality. In the article that follows Mr Adessa and Miss Laatsch describe how decisions about the visits of parents to their children are made in a treatment centre for seriously disturbed children, some of whom are psychotic. It is accepted that stress is inherent in all visiting, as the parents' presence may reactivate real or internalized conflicts which were the original cause of a child's admission, but it is also recognized that the prohibition of visiting creates stress of a different kind. The writers underline the necessity of studying the effect of parental visits in each case and deciding according to the personality strengths of each child both the frequency of parental visits and the form that they should take.

Most children in residential treatment centres have living parents whose direct and periodic contact with them through visiting may either aid or impede the course of therapy. Collateral treatment of parents, be it supportive or insightful, is a widely accepted accompaniment to the in-patient therapy of the child. Not yet clearly conceptualized are the therapeutic principles that are needed to guide the treatment institution in making the many decisions about visiting between parent and child.

'Visiting policies' indeed exist. Not infrequently they date from an earlier, less treatment-oriented phase in the centre's development and may no longer be compatible with current treatment objectives. The disparity between overall treatment intent and actual visiting practice can and does result in subtle but serious obstacles to treatment, with staff unable to pinpoint quite what went wrong, and why.

Should parents visit each week? Should they visit at all? Are visits to be restricted to the grounds? Under what conditions should the child visit home? What safeguards can the treatment agency enforce? These and similar questions recur insistently, plaguing all levels of staff. In the absence of clear guideposts, they tend to be answered inconsistently or in terms of staff convenience rather than on the basis of treatment objectives. Yet visiting arrangements solidly based and carried out with conviction and average competency are essential for therapeutic gain.

The special and vivid importance of visiting arises from the fact that it repeatedly confronts the child with the primary libidinal objects linked to his deepest conflicts. Aside from inherent constitutional factors, it is the quality and duration of the child's earliest object relationships with parent figures that largely established the terms on which subsequent life experiences were met and that ultimately necessitated the major step of placement in a residential treatment unit. Each visit reactivates the conflicts and ambivalence involved in the parent-child relationship. There is no doubt that visiting is emotionally supercharged for the child and the parents–and for staff as well. Issues involved in visiting, therefore, cannot safely be left to policy making that is not based on dynamic understanding of its meaning.

In this paper we attempt to draw some generalizations of therapeutic value from the viscissitudes of visiting as experienced and worked out at Lakeside Children's Centre.[1] Its population

[1] Lakeside Children's Centre provides residential treatment for seriously disturbed children. It is located on a five-acre plot in a middle-class neighbourhood of small homes and businesses. The neighbourhood is immediately adjacent to an older, wealthier section. The premises contain three cottages for children with a population of 6 girls and 24 boys. The children ranging in age from 6 to more than 18, live in five group units containing six children apiece. The child care counsellor staff consists of 22 men and women, the majority college educated, who are employed on a 45-hour week. Five psychiatric social workers are responsible for individual psychotherapy, and a child analyst serves as consultant. Most of the children at this treatment centre attend special classes of from one to five students in the school building on the grounds, the teachers being employed and assigned to the centre by the Milwaukee public schools.

consists mainly of youngsters with weak and fragmented egos who are seriously defective in adaptive capabilities. Early and pervasive psychic trauma, frequently accompanied by actual deprivation and physical abuse, characterizes the children's histories. Clinically, about one-fourth of the children are psychotic, most of the others have character disorders or are ego-defective, and a few are basically neurotic.

It is axiomatic that seriously damaged children cannot achieve sound ego growth in a short time. The process of residential treatment is that of ego building rather than only ego rebuilding; it is more habilitative than rehabilitative. Because treatment is lengthy, children reside at Lakeside for many years—only infrequently for less than four or five. With few exceptions, children stay for as long as their individual treatment requires. The agency is viewed by children, staff, and parents as that place where the children *live*, not as a temporary way station. They reside in long-term security at an institution that tries to fulfill most of their needs, protects them from disintegrating periods of stress, and provides opportunity for growth.

BASIC PRINCIPLES UNDERLYING VISITING

In residential treatment, individual psychotherapy, therapeutic education, and the child's daily living experiences together give him maximal opportunities to overcome severe developmental fixations so that growth processes may resume. All aspects of his life-in-residence are potentially capable of having therapeutic impact. It follows, then, that the timing, handling, and arrangements of all visits to the child fall within the treating agency's responsibility. Factors of plant design, staffing pattern, and controlling auspices may make for variations in visiting arrangements among treatment institutions, but the principles on which such plans need to be based remain the same.

The basic guiding principles are: (1) visiting must preclude such stress as triggers internal conflict, defensive behaviour, and ego disintegration that in magnitude and kind seriously impedes or prevents treatment (note that this formulation does not state that visiting either can or should obviate stress *per se*) and (2) visiting should maximize growth-producing aspects of the parent-child relationship.

Ego disintegration can best be minimized or avoided by anticipating stressful situations and then obviating them through the creative use of a variety of individualized arrangements. The centre has the prerogative of varying the frequency, the duration, and the locale of visiting, as well as the people involved in visiting. The sensitive use of this prerogative provides an important lever in treatment, making it possible for the visit to produce minimal or therapeutically workable amounts of stress.

HOW VISITING PRODUCES STRESS

Stress is inherent in all visiting. The longer the visit, the greater the frequency, the larger the number of people involved, and the greater the distance from the treatment centre, the more the stress potential that exists.

Even when parents are reasonably benign in their handling of the child during a visit, their very presence can reactivate the internalized conflict that originated in the earlier relationship. When this occurs, the modification of visiting arrangements can reduce stress until such time as the child comes to realize that he is responding to an internalized image rather than to his parents as they are at the moment. Treatment staff need to be aware of the distortion reactions on the part of the child, since, out of over-identification, staff may also tend to perceive the parents as bad or destructive. Direct observation of parent-child visiting by staff serves to act as a corrective measure for this propensity.

Unfortunately, visits that provide an opportunity for actual repetition of situations and interactions that contributed to the child's disturbance are the more common variety. The possibilities for acting out conflicts during a visit are almost infinite. The acting out may be initiated by either the child or the parents. For instance, a mother may stir up in a child a conflict of loyalties between the treatment agency and the parents. This can occur when, as a result of her own oral-dependent competitiveness with the child, the mother is outspokenly critical of clothing that the child has received, of the care given him, or of his therapist or his counsellor. Alternatively, the child may seek to engage his mother or his grandmother in rivalry with staff over his care when, for example, this has been his lifelong protective pattern against being totally ignored. Parents sometimes use the child as a pawn in their own battles. Thus, a corruptive father may unconsciously push his son into antisocial behaviour.

Stress in visiting comes about in many additional ways. A parent may be actually or potentially abusive, seductive, threatening, or depreciating toward a child. He may pass along information or gossip regarding family problems, which can often be upsetting or damaging to the child. A parent's inability during a visit to be giving, or meaningfully communicative, may well repeat earlier disappointments in the relationship. A parent who does not visit as promised, who arrives late or early, or who comes irregularly can also reinforce earlier severe disappointments. Bizarre or deviant behaviour on the part of a parent can be grossly embarrassing to the child. Sibling rivalry is easily revived, particularly if the brother or sister actually comes to visit. These are but a few of the stress-creating situations that reactivate conflict within a child.

Although visiting creates stress for children, it does not follow that it is to be entirely prohibited. A child may need reassurance that his anger has not killed his parents, that thay have not totally forgotten him, or that the treatment institution is not trying to deprive him of them. The elimination of visiting would produce its own stress. Consequently, more therapeutic potential exists in the variable handling of visiting arrangements than in the outright prohibition of visiting.

When visits are less frequent at the beginning of a child's stay the treatment centre can judge whether his behaviour following the visit results from the stress of the visit or whether it represents his general behavioural pattern. If a child was reacting to the recurrent stress of weekly visits with a week of regression after each one, it would be impossible to make this differentiation. Then, too, visiting begun on a weekly schedule only too frequently has to be limited eventually. It has been found that parents can tolerate restrictions on visiting best at the beginning of their child's placement. They tend to see limitations added later as deprivations meant to punish them for anger and destructive impulses toward the child or as a judgment of their adequacy as parents.

Immediately after admission it is most effective for a child to be visited on grounds, bi-weekly or monthly, for an hour or two each time. Although visits may be increased to a bi-weekly or a weekly basis after a year or so (actually, only two of the thirty children at Lakeside have weekly visits), some children continue to be visited by their parents on the original, limited schedule for much longer. In such cases, the children may themselves not wish for an increase in visiting, they may need protection from stress for a longer period of time, or their parents may practically or psychically not be able to visit more often. It is rare that visiting is reduced on the treatment centre's initiative to less than once a month. Sometimes, irregular and infrequent parental visiting is incorrectly viewed by the child as the centre's plan. In such cases it has occasionally been found helpful to place no limitation' on visiting, thereby having the child face the reality that it is actually his parents' decision to visit in a limited way.

When stress reduction for the child is necessary and a stringent visiting schedule (for example, once every three months) meets great resistance from the parents, the treatment centre has the alternative of modifying other variables. Restricting visits to the grounds of the institution is one possibility. The solid physical presence of the grounds and buildings can represent to both child and parents the centre's protection and authority. Further, the presence of child care counsellors nearby tends to inhibit stressful behaviour. With on-grounds visiting, the child need not feel the rage of an unpredictable parent to the same extent that he does away from the centre. And a mother's wearing two dresses and wondering if it is Easter in June will be more tolerable to her adolescent son if they visit within the confines of the centre than it would be if he had to anticipate being seen on the street with her.

It is possible for the counsellor, by plan, to sit in on the on-grounds visit discreetly or as an active participant. A psychotic mother with settled convictions about extra-sensory perception is less likely to confuse her child when a counsellor is there to help change the subject. The mere presence of a counsellor can discourage a mother's nagging and depreciating of her daughter while serving to support the mother's own basic wish to do what is most helpful for her child. Restricting a visit to the living-room of the cottage in the presence of counsellors protected one child from any threat of seduction by a father who had molested her when she was very young. The counsellor can also usefully structure a visit by suggesting some game or activity to the parent who finds conversation difficult or cannot easily initiate play with his child.

Visiting on grounds, particularly for the several months following admission, serves additional important purposes. It helps the child to realize that separation from the parents is real. It symbolically affirms that the treatment centre is now the responsible decision maker in the child's life and the provider of need gratification on which he must depend. It gives staff ample opportunity to observe the nature of the relationship between the child and his parents. Direct observation of the visits is particularly helpful in work with those children and parents who have much difficulty in talking of the visits and their feelings about them. The child care counsellor's comments about the mother who is withdrawn and uninterested in her child, or about the mother who talks of the superior accomplishments of the sibling, can then be used in individual therapy when a child brings in pertinent material. (About half of the children at Lakeside Children's Centre invariably remain on grounds with their parents.)

VISITING OFF GROUNDS OR AT HOME

A child should not be considered ready for off-grounds or home visits until the staff judges his ego sufficiently strong to be reasonably adaptive to the anticipated degrees of stress. Off-grounds visits clearly enhance the likelihood of stress; yet they are not all of a piece: for example, visiting a nearby drugstore has a lower probability of generating stress than going home for a full day's visit. Visiting off grounds precludes planned observations by treatment centre staff. Therefore, such arrangements imply that the agency expects the child or the parent to be capable of communicating later, in a relatively meaningful way, about both tangible and intangible aspects of the visit.

When the visit is off grounds, it is possible, because of the location of our treatment centre, for children to go to a nearby market, beach, park, or restaurant with their parents and yet be within very close range of the centre. An adolescent girl whose psychotic mother unexpectedly became involved in a street argument with another woman had only a block to go in fleeing back to her cottage. Parents and children who are better integrated, whose behaviour is more rather than less predictable, can venture on longer trips and more distant visits. They can go to the zoo, the museum, or the ball park or window shop at downtown department stores.

Careful planning with parents about the activities engaged in during off-grounds or at-home visits can forestall difficulty. For instance, it would be unwise for parents to go to the circus with a child who is tormented by fantasies of wild animals and who uses counterphobic defences. Similarly, a child who is fearful of his father's hostile aggressions could have a fine time fishing with him, but not hunting.

Short, close-by excursions, as well as on-grounds visits, are most typically planned to be an hour or two in duration. Special outings and events can be longer; they vary from an afternoon's trip to the museum to an all-day fishing excursion to a weekend visit home.

Visits to the parental home provide little or no protective control and can generate much stress. Therefore, the children permitted to visit their parents' home are those whose adaptive capabilities have been greatly strengthened and who have feelings of security in their relationship to the centre and to home. Home-visit stress can be minimized by short stays of one hour to four hours. Overnight and weekend visits are usually contraindicated unless the child's adaptive capabilities are reasonably able to withstand family pathology, be it gross or subtle. Only five children at Lakeside are currently visiting home with any regularity, though there may be occasional home visits planned for some of the others.

Generally speaking, a child's having ego strength compatible with at-home visiting implies that he is close to the end of his need for residential treatment and for the protective care it exercises. Consequently, overnight visiting tends to have primary value in the course of preparing both child and family for his impending return home, though this may be many months away. Home visits, overnight or less, may also be planned when it is considered therapeutically advisable for the child to be confronted with the reality of his parents' mode of living and family relationships. In other instances, for example, when a family has moved into a new house or a new neighbourhood, the counsellor or the child therapist may visit the home with the child, particularly if this will help the child to feel part of the family.

THE PEOPLE WHO VISIT

Parents should be the main figures in all visiting plans, since they are usually the most meaningful as well as the most ambivalent figures in the child's life. It is with the parents that the treatment centre works most closely in order to help them understand and deal with the behaviour of the child. If there have been other people of positive significance to the child, such as grandparents, they also visit on a regular basis. Distant relatives and family friends can visit by arrangement on an infrequent schedule. Siblings may or may not visit, depending on their meaning to the child in placement. Often, the child is under less stress if they visit infrequently and only by plan.

CHANGING PLAN TO REDUCE STRESS

Despite all precautions that may be taken to ensure that stress-producing elements of a visit are kept to a minimum, one may often see what is most frequently described as 'upset' behaviour by a child after a visit. It is highly important that all residential treatment staff be alert to such behavioural patterns, particularly since the child himself may be quite unaware of, or deny their relationship to, affect stirred up by the visit. Staff assessment may help determine whether a change in visiting arrangements is necessary.

The criteria for evaluating visiting stress are the type, the degree, and the length of the child's defensive reactions and ego disintegration. When there is a serious intensification of symptomatic behaviour after a visit, it can be assumed that anxiety has been aroused with which the child could not deal in a suitably adaptive fashion, and thus he handles with maladaptive defences. These defences, of course, may be present in varying degrees at all times.

When they are intensified by visits and persist in aggravated fashion over a long period of time, thereby seriously interfering with growth processes, an effort must be made to reduce the stress caused by the visiting.

A psychotic boy of latency age withdrew into a long fantasy, and his behaviour became extremely compulsive for four or five days after each weekly visit with his mother. When visits were reduced to once a month, the regressive behaviour reactive to the visits became but a minor portion of his functioning, and he was able to make a steady push toward healthier modes of adaptive behaviour.

Another child displayed increased hyper-activity for several hours after weekly visits with parents, and sometimes even prior to each visit. In this instance, however, the child's reaction could be worked with in individual therapy and therefore did not call for a change in the visiting schedule. The child was helped to handle his anxiety by making him aware of its relationship to the impending visit.

Persistently demanding, pestering behaviour on the part of another child was noted for several days after each weekly visit. Again, visiting was reduced, and the parents were requested to come without the child's envied sibling. The child care counsellors soon noticed a longer span of better-integrated behaviour.

Still another psychotic youngster displayed increased head banging and a much lower frustration tolerance after brief off-grounds visits with co-operative parents. A return to on-grounds visiting led to diminution of the regressive behaviour.

CHILDREN'S REACTIONS TO VISITING

At times, one notices in reaction to visiting certain behaviour that is indicative of guilt in a particular child: for example, being provocative, handling responsibilities so poorly that restrictions on activities must surely follow, or avoiding therapy sessions. In one instance, a parent was stirring up guilt in a child by creating a conflict of loyalties, acting out through him, and generally disrupting his treatment. In that situation, the duration rather than the frequency of visits was reduced. The child was told that if he was able to cope with the stress his mother produced, the centre would have no objection to the longer visits, but since his behaviour showed that they were too much for him, limitations were necessary. Although the problem was by no means promptly resolved, this procedure did help the boy take a major step in understanding how his mother acted out her own problems through him.

Sometimes aggressive, provocative behaviour is a child's defence against experiencing the loss of self-esteem that an unhappy visit has stirred up in him. Such loss may be the result of anything from a parent's utter inadequacy in giving psychically to the child to the flaunting of the virtues of a sibling before him. Some children, on the other hand, will be more conforming and isolated after an unhappy visit with parents, as a result of increased fear of the loss of their love.

There is great variety both in the content of specific conflicts that are triggered in children by parental visits and in the consequent defensive manoeuvring in which they engage. Treatment staff must know the defensive patterns of a particular child in order to be able to judge whether a given sequence of behaviour, be it greater difficulty in learning or extreme temper tantrums, may have been set off by the visit. Any piece of maladaptive defensive behaviour that results from a visit and persists for an extended period of time, so as to interfere with a child's treatment, would certainly indicate the need for a thorough review and possible revision of visiting arrangements. This does not mean that change is initiated suddenly. It sometimes takes a considerable period of time to become aware that the defensive behaviour may be connected with the visiting. It may also take some time to test out that hypothesis. When major changes in visiting arrangements have to be made, a thorough understanding of the relationship between the visits and the child's regressive behaviour enables staff to meet in a helpful way the parental opposition that can arise.

If a child can express feelings about visits, can use his observations and reactions to further understanding of himself, and can grow from these experiences, the treatment centre does not try to protect him from all pain or stress.

Tom, an adolescent, went home for his first visit in four years. He had not seen his parents in more than three months. He was deeply disappointed at finding the family and home much the same as he had known them. Although he returned proclaiming great pleasure in the visit, within a few days there was return of much earlier symptomatology, deterioration in school work, regressive relationship with peers, and renewed manipulative behaviour with adults. As Tom was helped to become aware of his reaction to the visits, he was able to let himself know about the affect involved and the conflicts stirred up.

After several weeks, he did regain a more mature integration. When he was later invited to attend the wedding of an older sister, he expressed the desire to go. After the pros and cons of the matter had been explored with him, he was allowed to attend. This time the way he handled the situation resulted in minimal after-effects, and he was proud of his heightened capacity to cope with it. Thus, for this boy, at his particular level of integration, the first visit home was a significant learning and mastering experience.

WORK WITH PARENTS

The effectiveness of a visiting arrangement is obviously influenced by the extent to which the parents are able to understand the limitations established by the treatment centre and to co-operate in planning. This in turn is made possible by the parents' relationship to, and work with, their therapist. Their co-operation in the visiting arrangements is one important way in which the parents more actively participate in the child's treatment. (Some parents who do not wish to visit frequently find it helpful to have the centre relieve them of guilt; the centre will 'take the blame' when this is in the child's best interests.)

At the centre, casework with the parents is usually carried on by the child's therapist. The foundation for co-operation over visiting arrangements is laid, however, at the time of the pre-admission study. The reasons for initial visiting arrangements, as well as the inability to know or to promise what future arrangements may be, are thoroughly explained. No encouragement is given to expect frequent visits. It should be noted that these matters are discussed with the parents before they make the final decision to place the child.

In order to maximize the growth-producing potential in the parent-child relationship, parents must also be helped to understand the child's behaviour and their own behaviour in relation to him. For instance, a mother and father were helped to understand why, in the course of visits, they should discourage their son's apparently self-sufficient behaviour, such as treating the family to a soda. The child really needed the constant reassurance that everyone would care for him, even though his defensive pattern was to deny the fear of abandonment by acting more grown-up and independent. Another mother and father were helped to see that their son's request to have them say goodbye to him by shaking hands was not a sign of withdrawal and distancing, but rather of his greater maturity.

When parents, through the casework services given them, have developed a generally positive, co-operative relationship with the agency, they become able to use the examples and guidance of the child care staff to make visiting a more positive experience for them and the child. Thus, a father was receptive and not threatened when a child care counsellor provided a ball and bat so that he could play with his son when it was observed that the two were uncomfortable with each other during the visit. Parents may also be helped to learn to play cards or to become acquainted with a new table game that the child enjoys. In another case, a counsellor provided the opportunity for a child to show off her increased skill at the piano and guided the parents into appropriately complimenting her when they could not do so on their own. After listening to the meandering tales of a psychotic mother, a counsellor provided cookies and milk for her and her child in order to give the two a means for overt relating. A father was able to be more patient with his autistic son, who ignored him, after the counsellor had demonstrated a way of attracting his attention. She encouraged the boy to turn his head toward the father, who had a balloon ready to help catch the child's eye. On the whole, unassuming demonstrations of ways of dealing with a child can help parents alter their own methods slightly during a visit, while giving the therapist further opportunity to deal with the underlying attitudes that have made it impossible for the parents to use such methods themselves earlier.

THE DECISION-MAKING PROCESS

At Lakeside, final decisions concerning visiting arrangements rest with the child's therapist. But all staff involved with the child gather information, provide observations, and give opinions before the decision is made. Such mutual cross-checking guards against preconscious and unconscious motivations that may bias a decision. For example, denials of parental requests may arise out of rivalry with the parents, while assents to requests for more liberal visiting arrangements may result from over-estimating the child's strengths as an assurance to oneself of the effectiveness of therapy. Further, persistent pressure by parents and children in regard to visiting can push a therapist to make a decision without fully attending to certain facts of the case. The more that staff is aware of the dynamic reasons for, and the principles underlying, visiting arrangements, the more confidence there will be both in the decisions made about visiting and in the evaluation of the resultant stress.

Sylvester Adessa has been Director of Lakeside Children's Centre, Milwaukee, Wisconsin since 1954 and Audrey Laatsch has been on the staff as therapist amd then as Director of Therapy since 1959. Sylvester Adessa studied economics and sociology at Queens College, New York and gained his degree in social work at the University of Chicago. He has had experience in community organization and as a psychiatric social worker.

Audrey Laatsch studied social work at the University of Wisconsin and psychiatric social work at the University of California, School of Social Work, Berkeley. Before coming to Lakeside Children's Centre she was a caseworker for children with difficult problems at the Wisconsin State Department of Public Welfare, Division for children and youth.

6

The problem of making adaptation to the needs of the individual child in a group

'New Trends in Child Care' *The Magazine of the R.C.C.A.*, vol. 9, 1961.

B. E. Dockar-Drysdale

Here is an article to read twice, first to absorb Mrs Dockar-Drysdale's concerned sensitivity or empathy for unhappy children and then to look more carefully at the distinction she makes between adaption to demands and adaptation to expectations (an acknowledged refinement on dictionary usage). She brings these contrasting situations home to us by comparing them to the different stages of a mother's relationship to her own child, adaption to the demands of the new-born baby, adaptation to meet the expectations of the growing child. She also surprises us with her suggestion that our own failure to meet the needs of a child, provided we can face and understand it, can be an opportunity to help a child painfully to recognize his own separate identity. The idea of 'concerned neglect' may also be a reassuring one to those of us who are deeply aware of children's needs, yet, do what we will, cannot meet them all the time. The story of the boy and the poem about the centipede repays unravelling and may remind you of other occasions when we have been aware of communicating with a child in a veiled or symbolic way; in the next article Mrs Winnicott helps us to think and feel more deeply about the purpose of communication and the means of communicating.

The problem of meeting the needs of individual children in a group situation is one which everybody who works closely with children must experience sooner or later. It is one of the most difficult and frustrating situations in residential work to find oneself, having established contact with a particular child on an individual basis, unable to carry this over into life in the group. The opportunities for work with individual children are usually few and far between, so that it is only too easy for the fragile bond between grown-up and child to be broken in the stress and strain of the group situation before it is even really established. Such a state of things is, of course, extremely bad for the child concerned, and equally disastrous for the grown-up. Is it possible to manage to strengthen such a bond despite all the obvious difficulties involved?

I am not in this paper discussing the very special form of adaption belonging to one phase of a total regression, which, in any case, I call conscious involvement rather than adaption and have discussed elsewhere. I felt that it would only be confusing to consider involvement in the context of group work because the deepest phase of a total regression must take place between a grown-up and a child with emotional support, and is something very different from anything which can take place in a group.

I am not discussing group therapy because that is work which I would feel to be dependent on a nucleus of ego strength in some or all members of the group, on which the therapist can depend. It would be impossible, for example, to do real group therapy with psychotic children, although a therapist could be working with several psychotic children who happened to be in one room at the same time. In the same way children who have had little or no opportunity for satisfactory emotional experience may seem to be together in a group, but are really utterly isolated from each other, with no inner resources to pool with those of the therapist. It is adaption to the needs of this kind of child that I am considering.

The mother with a new-born baby is in a state of unity; she is for the time being, also, in a state of near perfect adaption to her baby, she does not have to *make* an adaptation deliberately; there is no conflict, no problem involved, because what the baby needs is what she needs.

A grown-up living in a residential setting with a group of children, cannot, and in fact should not, become adapted in this sort of way, although this might be precisely what is being demanded of the grown-up by the child. I think this is often a very hard fact to face, because it may easily be that the grown-up may feel a great need to cede to a child's demands, to become involved in a situation comparable to a mother with her new-born baby, because this state of adaption is a deeply satisfying state of things – at all events at first, for grown-up and child; especially because the grown-up is able to feel that he, or she, is giving the child all it needs, and the child is feeling that, at least, here is everything, the whole world, the universe – his for the taking – and more and more and more.

Now, I have watched this sort of process take place in residential treatment, and such stories do not have a happy ending for anybody concerned. Very soon there is intense resentment felt by other members of the staff who are not themselves in a state of adaption, and do not wish to be, and who feel – in fact, quite rightly – that there is something which is not quite right about such a situation, which tends to be extremely disruptive to both other grown-ups and other children.

Presently, also, the adapted grown-up reaches the limits of endurance, and suddenly feels that he, or she, is losing identity and becoming lost in the child, whose demands become more and more omnipotent. At the same time the child becomes panicky, because as one child said to me recently, 'Everything is really the same as nothing, and if I get absolutely everything there would be nothing at all.'

At this stage several things can happen. The grown-up may suddenly withdraw from the situation having become suddenly aware of a need for self-preservation; or may modify his or her attitude and refuse to meet demands; or, in order to keep the whole thing going, the grown-up and the child may isolate themselves in a little world of their own, regarding everybody else as enemies; or the grown-up may have some sort of physical collapse. One thing is sure, and that is that infinite adaption to the demands of such a child is an impossibility, and the various breakdowns which I have described lead to chaos for everybody in the environment, because when something of this sort happens, the child, in a frenzied panic, destroys everything within reach. I know that I have painted a gloomy picture here, but I feel that there is a very real danger that people working with children can under-value what they are doing because they feel that to be therapeutic is to be permissive and that they are all the time falling short of what is needed, whereas, in fact, they are probably doing extremely well and giving a great deal of help to children.

I think we must all face the fact–whatever our particular work may be–that we are not going to be able to give a child everything he needs all the time. It would also be true to say that this applies to mothers with their babies, and that failure to meet needs becomes an important factor in emotional growth, and that while failure in adaptation is inevitable we need never 'let a child down' which is something quite different.

So far I have spoken about *adaption to demands* and the dangers attending this: now I wish to consider *adaptation to meet expectations*, which is something very different. (I must make it clear at this point that there is no such distinction in the dictionary, where adaption and adaptation have the same meaning.)

I have referred already to the state of adaption in which a mother exists with her new-born baby (in a supporting element– the environment, father, other family, etc.).

The next stage reached is where a normal mother, deliberately and aware, but without inner stress, is able to meet her baby's needs, as it slowly establishes itself as a separate integrated person. The baby's needs will not now be necessarily her own, but she will be so aware of these needs that she will supply them at once with a minimum of delay or hesitation–it will be natural to do this. She does not have to think about this sort of thing, she does it spontaneously, 'with her eyes shut'. The baby, this stage having been reached, having had this sort of experience, has expectations and although now and then she will fail to meet them, she will be sufficiently reliable for it to be unnecessary for the baby to *fall back on demands*, which are then *failed expectations*.

If the expectations are met and all goes well, there may still be demands, but the mother may refuse these, more often than not, thus enabling the baby to get angry with her–and it is important for this to be possible.

On the other hand she will continue to make adaptation to needs, gradually failing as this becomes less necessary. So that eventually there remain only the token adaptations which mothers make to their children's needs even when they are quite grown-up (a special nickname, a kind of hot drink, a funny little joke). Such token adaptations are in addition to those which any mature person makes to the needs of other individuals and of society as a whole.

Now if things go wrong, which can happen for the many reasons we all know, the resulting history is very different, and produces the kind of child about whom we are so worried.

Because his needs have not been met he has no expectations and can only make demands. What we then have to create is a state of things in which, his needs having been fulfilled, he is, at last, in a position to have expectations. We cannot take such a child back to search for something he has lost, we have to take him forward to discover something he has never known.

So far so good. What are the needs of a baby? Soft breast, warm milk, holding arms and all the rest. How can we hope to provide these things for a tough ten-year-old? And suppose that we *can* produce a fairly satisfactory experience for one child, how can we hope to provide a similar experience for a whole group all apparently with the same needs. Here 'apparently' is the key word. A child said to me recently, 'Fair play wouldn't be any use to people like us, because it would only mean that we'd all get the same thing and each of us needs something different.'

Peter, when he came to us, demanded everything the whole time, and it was important that we should be able to say 'No' to his demands, and yet remain concerned about him. (A 'no' without rejection.) He always demanded the *whole* tin of biscuits, *all* our attention—*everything*. He did not, however, allow us to do anything for him, to look after him or comfort him, he had terrible rages, panics and fits of despair—he was never sad, or frightened, or anxious. Gradually he became deeply dependent on one person—a first experience of love, because he had never reached the stage of really loving somebody—and he made it clear to this loved person that she could take care of his nose—his little, helpless nose. Now, up to this point he had been a child with a nose which was always in need of a blow—rather disgusting. A helpless little nose was of course another matter. His grown-up layed in a special stock of handkerchief tissues, and took care of Peter's nose. His demands grew less as his expectations became established and gradually he and his grown-up found other ways of feasible care-taking, other practical means of making adaptations to his particular needs.

Another small boy who started by demanding all things bright and beautiful and everything else, settled for a piece of buttered toast each morning–buttered by his therapist at the end of staff breakfast. (For various reasons we have our meals after the children.) This, day after day, and month after month.

The important point about such adaptations is that they have to be really possible to make, and to continue to make, as long as they are necessary–which, after all, is what a mother does, only for us it is a technique to be used in our work while for her it is part of her own private life. Often there is quite a long period during which the child experiments–seeking for something 'which will really work'. It is important that the grown-up should not consent to make an adaptation which cannot be sustained for a period, because reliability is the most important single attribute required in such work. The most essential thing the grown-up can do is to survive, 'to be there in the morning' with something to give, something to take and something to keep for his or herself.

It is interesting to see the understanding that other children show in regard to adaptation to needs (whereas they savagely resent adaption to demands). Recently a child was discussing with me in a group the possibility of a supply of potato crisps to be kept by his therapist so that he could have a packet from time to time. Another child–a newcomer–asked whether everyone would have this, and an experienced member of the group aged about nine explained, 'No, crisps would be right for him; there'll be something you'll find that's right for you, like John who has that special sort of cereal, it really matters to him.'

I have spoken about failure in adaptation having its place in emotional development, and, of course, we are bound–sooner or later–to fail in our adaptations to children's needs. Probably many of you have read some of Dr Winnicott's important papers; he points out the tremendous use which can be made of such failures in the here-and-now situation. It is essential that one should not explain away such failures, but that they should be recognized and acknowledged by grown-up and child, so that the child can at last experience the appropriate anger–the anger which should have been felt in babyhood at the time of the original failure–the time when, as one child said to me recently, 'the wind blew, the bough broke, the cradle fell'.

A child can see astonishing things as failures, and I think this often explains their apparently irrational accusations against the people they love and on whom they depend. The absence of the loved person, whatever the reason and however well prepared the child may be, can be such a failure; or the grown-up's failure to understand something which, anyhow, the child has not said, or understanding something too quickly. It is extraordinary how possible it is for a child going through such an experience with a grown-up to find everything needed in the stuff of everyday existence.

Only when such a failure in adaptation is fully understood by the grown-up and the child, does it become valuable to put it right. What can happen too easily is that the grown-up may feel such a need to make restitution to the child that failure does not get used.

Quite apart from maintained arrangements there are single adaptations which may be very dramatic.

One such occasion in my own experience was when I took a child out with me, with whom I had a very close bond, and who was extremely dependent upon me at that point. I had to go to Oxford and to do various things in the course of the afternoon, and found myself with no time left to use for something special with James, as I had counted on being able to do. We walked up the High Street together, which as some of you may know is very long and usually very crowded; it certainly was on this particular afternoon. I was wondering to myself what I could possibly do that would meet James's needs and be something just for him, when I noticed that he was walking more and more slowly. I was not sure what this was about, so I fortunately did not make any comment, but presently James dropped some distance behind me, and then proceeded up The High at a snail's pace, regardless of jostling crowds, and the fact that we were already late.

I decided that he wanted to lose me, and find me again, or something like that, so at first I just kept steadily on, although continuing to be aware of his whereabouts. However, when presently he stopped moving altogether and simply stood in the middle of the crowd, I realized that I was not understanding. I threaded my way back to him, and waited without saying anything until he started to move again, which he presently did, walking more slowly than I would have believed possible for this particularly agile, lively, and independent child. It suddenly dawned on me that this was the means he had found for me to make the necessary adaptation: here was the little child just beginning to walk, whose mother suits her pace to his, and is quite prepared to take all the time in the world in order that her child can have the experience of walking by himself—but with the support of her presence. There was a very real problem involved for me in this situation, because I find it extremely hard to walk slowly anyhow, knew we were late, and knew also, that unless I could really feel that this was the most important thing for James and for me, however slowly I walked, it would be of no use to him. He didn't even wish to speak (neither of us had said a word about all this) and we were making this long and exhausting journey in absolute silence. I decided that the best hope was for me to notice the architecture in The High (which normally I don't have time to do), providing that I could still remain concerned with James. This worked very well, and made the slow pace more tolerable for me. When we eventually reached the top of the street, James, without comment, suddenly returned to his normal speed, and shot down Cornmarket Street like an arrow, but he was extremely happy and contented, and I knew that something important had happened for him, as indeed it had happened for me.

There are certain times when one is especially aware of the necessity of adaptation to individual needs, one such occasion is bedtime; a story read to the whole group, although valuable in other ways does not fulfil this special purpose, and it is difficult to find a way of giving each child an individual experience. Of course this will depend on the particular grown-up and children concerned—everybody has their own special way of doing things, which is the only way that will be satisfactory—personally I rely on what the children call 'mouse parties' and 'perches'.

'Mouse parties' usually mean a bag of sultanas, and the adaptation here consists quite simply in giving a few sultanas to each child. Nothing, however, could be more different than the way in which various children need to receive such a 'mouse party'. One child likes to be given his sultanas one at a time, saying over each sultana, 'That's not much', until suddenly he cries, 'That's enough.' Another child needs to be able to say, 'I don't like sultanas, anyhow'. And the correct response to this is to put his collection of sultanas on the little table by his bed, where he collects it subsequently. Another child holds out his cupped hands into which I must let fall about six sultanas, whereupon he says, 'A little more', and then, 'a little more', and so on until finally he says, 'one more', and that is enough!

There are endless variations and it is important that I remember exactly what each child needs. A fascinating fact is that all the children do get about the same number of sultanas, it is the way in which they receive them which makes the 'mouse party' an individual and special experience.

'Perches' involve my sitting on the side of each bed in turn for a very few minutes; and here again each child uses these few minutes in a special and highly individual way. One child plays a complicated finger game with one of my hands and his own hands. Another child likes me to sing him a French song. Another child always uses this time to tell me something about what he feels it was like inside his mother before he was born. Here again I am often completely amazed by the tremendous use which they make of a few minutes, and I am also very impressed by the respect with which 'perches' are regarded. Children are prepared to wait for their turn and do not interrupt other children's 'perches' if they can help it.

There is another kind of adaptation which I call for convenience 'communication'; this is a valuable means of meeting individual needs in or out of a group–a lifeline between the grown-up and the child.

Communication, again, is something which mothers establish with their babies at quite an early stage, understanding intuitively the deeper inside meaning of what the child is saying, and responding in the medium which the child has chosen.

Understanding grown-ups working and playing with children use this kind of communication probably without even noticing that this is what they are doing. Perhaps some of the best work that any of us achieve is that which we understand the least–indeed I think our successes are often more surprising than our failures.

An example of communication was with a boy who had been extremely delinquent, had made a recovery, returned home, and was getting on quite well in a state of extreme dependence on his mother. For various reasons he tried to revert to the earlier pattern

and found he could no longer be successfully delinquent. He said
to me, 'In school a few days ago, I heard a very good poem.' The
poem was as follows:

> 'A centipede was happy quite,
> Until a toad in fun
> Said, "Pray which leg comes after which?"
> Which sent him into such a pitch
> He lay distracted in a ditch,
> Considering how to run.'

I said gravely that I did not think the toad had been in fun at
all, that while the centipede was happy he had indeed been running along very fast without his front leg knowing where his back
leg was going, and that the toad had, in fact, tried to teach him
how to walk. 'Did the centipede', I asked, 'really need to lie kick-
ing in the ditch considering how to run? Had he thought of
walking instead?' Edward said that it was mean of the toad to
make him think about his feet. I said that I thought it quite fair
that the centipede should feel angry with the toad, especially if the
centipede started the old running and suddenly found he could not
do it any more, just because he knew which foot was which.

The adaptations to needs which I am sure you all make again
and again, depend on concern, on therapeutic skill, on having an
emotional economy, on being reliable: if to all these you choose to
add theoretical knowledge, so much the better, but without the
essentials theoretical knowledge is of little use, and of all these
essentials reliability seems to be the most important, because it is in
your survival that the child will find expectations.

Lately we have come to understand something at the Bush which
has been of value to us and might be to you. This is a concept of
'concerned neglect'. You will all know the feeling of personal guilt
which one has when it is impossible to meet the very real needs of
one or more children in a group—in fact one is really neglecting
them. The important thing is I think that both you and the children should realize that this is so, that you *are* neglecting them . . .
but at the same time that you are aware of this and continuing to
feel concerned about them. We find that this is well worth stating
to the children in the actual context of the situation, so that one
may say to the child, 'I am terribly sorry. I should be with you

and helping you . . . or whatever, and I am not because I am doing something else, but I am going on being worried about you.' No reassuring here, no covering up of one's own personal guilt; this gives the child real assurance of your continued concern for him. I am sure that mothers with big families do this all the time. I often hear people say, 'I cannot imagine how a mother manages with her three or four children, all small, and all needing her at the same time . . .', and I feel that as well as the individual adaptations she makes to each child's needs and meeting of their expectations, there is also this condition of 'concerned neglect' from time to time, which she and they can face and understand and which she is not afraid to state.

Adaptions, which you will remember I discussed in the first place, will have its moments, there are instants for all of us when we can experience the sense of unity which belongs to the period just after birth; sometimes this will be when we are listening to music, or looking at a beautiful landscape, or experiencing something very deep with somebody else, a grown-up or child. And, in working with children there will be moments when we are completely involved and it is possible for an instant for child and grown-up to recapture what that earliest experience must have been. What we cannot do is to hold this, to try and maintain it, because this is an illusion and while illusions are terribly valuable they cannot be held and used; they are like the fairy gold which turns into dead leaves.

Adaptation, of course, also creates in some ways an illusion; but there is enough reality for this to be tested, so that it can really be used to help the child to experience something essential which he, or she, has never known. Perhaps one of the most valuable things we can do for such children is to give them something to lose, since only through loss are they likely to realize experience.

Barbara Dockar-Drysdale's interest in children in need of help began during the war, when her husband was serving abroad, and evacuated families and children came to the Berkshire village where she lived. She started a play group for these children, added some of them as boarders to her own family of four children, and this enterprise gradually grew into a residential school for maladjusted children, called the Mulberry Bush from the name of the original play group. The school is now recognized as a special school by the Department of Education and Science and receives severely disturbed children in need of residential treatment.

Mrs Dockar-Drysdale is a member of the Association of Psychotherapists and acts as therapeutic adviser both to the Mulberry Bush School and to the Cotswold Community near Ashton Keynes. A collection of her papers entitled Therapy in Child Care was published as volume 3 in this series in 1968. A further collection of papers will be published shortly entitled Consultation in Child Care.

7
Communicating with children

Child Care Quarterly Review, vol. 18, no. 3, 1964.

Clare Winnicott

Communicating with children, as Mrs Winnicott shows, is very much more than talking to children; it involves how we get on with children, how we make relationships with them, in fact it is the way to successful and satisfying care and caring. The aim of communication, she suggests, is to keep alive a child's capacity to feel. Many of the shared experiences of residential life, walks, playing, even watching TV may be opportunities for indirect communication and may lead on to direct communication of feeling. But we have probably all met children in residential care with whom it has been difficult to make real effective contact. Mrs Winnicott suggests that in such cases more careful and sensitive assessment is needed and she provides as a guide to this an analysis of five kinds of case. These cases include most of the hurt and resentful children, whom we meet in residential care, and Mrs Winnicott's descriptions tell us not only how we may be able better to communicate with them but also reveal some of the meaning of their behaviour. Here is an article to consult again when next we are troubled over a child who appears unable to accept what we so much want to give.

The article was based on a paper given by Mrs Winnicott at a meeting of the South-east Region of the Association of Child Care Officers in March 1964.

Suppose that we could agree that a rough definition of communication would be that it is quite simply a matter of giving and taking between people. A moment of communication is a moment of reciprocal exchange. The essential ingredient of communication is, of course, the will and the ability to communicate, and these depend on the individual's balance of trust and suspicion, which in turn depends on what is stored up in his or her inner world of the unconscious memories of previous communications, including the very earliest, and on his or her ability to use symbols. A symbol is simply something that is allowed to stand for something else. Words and gifts are symbols which have their own accepted meaning, but we who use them give them meaning over and above their literal content by the way in which we select them and use them. Words and other symbols can also be used defensively to hide ourselves and our feelings and to come between us and other people. But this is in itself a form of communication showing that we are unwilling or unable to communicate.

The capacity for symbol formation in the individual is an important part of normal development, and is a crucial matter in the capacity to communicate and to become socialized.

Put briefly a symbol is a secondary phenomenon which can be accepted and allowed to stand for a primary one, so that the primary one can be relinquished temporarily, and later permanently, as it becomes part of the phenomena and processes of everyday life. To put this in its simplest terms the infant, whose primary needs for food and care are continuously met in a way reliable enough to bring him satisfaction and a sense of well-being, stores up memories of these experiences and becomes able to fill the gaps in care, when mother is not actively caring for him, by finding pleasure and satisfaction in other things—the blanket or the woolly toy or whatever is available, his own thumb perhaps, or a dummy. This other thing gives satisfaction because it stands for the primary satisfactions and keeps alive memories of them. But there is more to it than this, because the other thing stands, at one and the same time, for the satisfaction-seeking infant and the mother who satisfies. The blanket or the woolly toy is therefore a symbol of unity between the self and the not-self and is evidence that the first vital link is being made between the infant and the outside world. Later the word 'mum-mum-mum' will be used to stand for the satisfying experience and the caring person, who is gradually recognized as a person. And so a whole new area for communication is opened up, based on the medium of words, which have to be learned. But this use of language will only go on developing if primary needs go on being met by the person who is the embodiment of the words. No wonder then that small children, and even older ones, separated from their mothers, so often lose the capacity for speech, or lose the sense of the meaning behind the words. It is only by sensitive patient care that the words will be given meaning again, but this will take time. If there is not good enough care then the words, although fluent, will remain meaningless, and serve only to come between the child and other people. The words will no longer be a vehicle for communication and moreover previous good experiences, and the stored memories of them, which represent the inner world and true self, will remain cut off from present feelings and everyday life and growth will be impoverished or distorted.

Our task, therefore, with children in this position is first to see that the day-by-day care of them is not merely adequate, but is as fully geared to their individual needs as it can be, because this is the basis for preserving, restoring, or establishing the capacity for real communication, real giving and taking.

It seems to me important that we social workers should remind ourselves that in the kind of communication that we hope to establish with children we are always cashing in on the work of others, on the work of those who have cared in the past, and those who are caring in the present, for the children's basic, day-to-day needs. The quality of this care will determine to quite a large extent the relative success or failure of anything that we can do.

I think we would agree that communication between people takes place on different levels of existence or experience. There is the ordinary everyday exchange between people which may take place on a somewhat superficial level, but nevertheless it serves to keep communication channels open, and has an important binding and socializing effect. It keeps civilization going, and the world ticking for us all, because it reduces suspicion and the latent paranoia in us all.

Then there is the communication, the prototype of which I have already described, which takes place between certain people and in which the feelings and needs of each are recognized and reciprocated. The true self of each meets and responds to the true self of the other.

The third kind of communication is that which concerns the exchange of ideas either in words or in art forms of all kinds. This is, at its best, a sophisticated elaboration and extension of the true self communication; at its worst it can be an attempt to hide the true self, and even to become a substitute for it. Strictly speaking when this happens communication is not taking place, although it may seem to be. What is said or painted on to canvas is then the private concern of one person—and the world guesses.

We know that when we are in communication with other people not only does it take place on different levels, but different ways will be used to convey meaning. What the voice *says* will only be part of the story, and sometimes the least important part. The rest will be in terms of attitude, posture, tone, gesture, look or touch—or the non-verbal signs and sounds we all make when what we feel will not go into words.

Then, too, often the things not said speak more loudly than the words said. For example, a woman patient in a hospital said to the Almoner: 'This has been a good year for roses, I wonder what they will be like next year.'[1] The real communication here was not about roses, but concerned the patient's knowledge that she would not live to see them next year. It was this knowledge that she wanted to communicate. Or another example would be that of a child being moved from one home to another who said to the Child Care Officer: 'Did David cry when he went away?' The real communication here was not about David, it was quite simply: 'I want to cry *now.*'

For those who would be in communication with others simply everything counts, and all our faculties are needed if we are to receive and interpret with approximate accuracy what others are expressing in what they are, or what they do and say. Fortunately experience increases our awareness of what people communicate and how they do it, but nevertheless we find that each case presents a new task in understanding simply because each individual is unique.

In order to reduce this fascinating but vast subject of communication with children to manageable proportions, I shall confine what I have to say to three aspects of it. The first is to try to put briefly into words what we are *aiming* at in communicating with children. Then, secondly, to raise questions concerning how we communicate, and thirdly to spend some time in discussing five kinds of cases which present special problems in communication.

With regard to the question of what we are aiming to achieve in

---

[1] Quoted from 'Communication with the patient', by Helen M. Lambrick. *The Almoner*, vol. 15, no. 7, October, 1962.

communicating with children, I would say first of all that we are not *aiming* to collect information or to take a case history, although of course we do all the time incidentally collect information about the children and gradually piece together their life story as seen by themselves. This is important to us, and to the children, because it helps us in our assessment of their problems, and it helps them to become aware of continuity. But behind this, our real aim is to keep children alive, and to help them to establish a sense of their own identity and worth in relation to other people. By keeping children alive I am of course referring to maintaining their capacity to feel. If there are no feelings there is no life, there is merely existence. All children who come our way have been through painful experiences of one kind or another, and this has led many of them to clamp down on feelings and others of them to feel angry and hostile, because this is more tolerable than to feel loss and isolation. Our work, therefore, is not easy because it will lead us to seek contact with the suffering part of each child, because locked up in the suffering is each one's potential for living and for feeling love as well as feeling hate and anger. To feel a sense of loss implies that something of value, something loved, is lost, otherwise there would be no loss. Awareness of loss therefore restores the value of that which is lost, and can lead in time to a reinstatement of the lost person and loving feelings in the inner life of the child. When this happens, real memories, as opposed to fantasies, of good past experiences can come flooding back and can be used to counteract the disappointments and frustrations which are also part of the past. In this way the past can become meaningful again. So many of the children we meet have no sense of the past and therefore they have no sense of the present and of the future. The child who has reached his or her own loving potential is then in a position to discover new loving relationships in the present and the future. If we attempt to reassure children and to jog them out of their despair we can deprive them of the chance to reach their own potential, i.e. to reach the love they were capable of before they suffered loss.

I now want to turn to the question of *how we set about* trying to get into touch with a child's real feelings. We find that usually it is no good if we set about this task in a deliberate way by trying to delve into the child's inner world because we shall be resisted if we do. The question and answer method simply does not work, and, moreover, we recognize that children have a right to their privacy, and only as we gain experience in implicitly recognizing this can we hope to gain their confidence. We know that we must relax, and see first that we adequately fulfil our rôle in relation to the children. Our rôle will be broadly determined by the nature of the responsibilities we carry on behalf of our agency. This will need to be made clear so that the child gradually comes to know what he or she may expect of us, and who we are and why we are there anyway.

Then within our rôle there is the question of what we ourselves are like as people. Do we talk to the grown-ups and ignore the child, or do we ignore the grown-ups and make an immediate fuss of the child in an attempt to evoke a response at all costs? Do we give time to the child and do we also give our undivided attention? Are we reliable? Do we keep promises, or do we forget? Are we the cheerful type, or the quiet type, and are we the same every time? There is a great deal about us as people that children need to establish, and they, even more than grown-ups, are quick to find us out, but this they must do if they are to know how to use us.

As I suggested earlier, real communication which involves direct giving and taking between people does not go on all the time. It happens at certain moments and with certain people and on the whole we select very carefully the people with whom we communicate in the deepest sense which involves our real feelings. Communication involves giving away a bit of ourselves and we are careful to whom we give it. Usually the people with whom we communicate are those whom we have come to trust and with whom we have something in common. In our work with children we therefore find that we spend a good deal of time creating the conditions which make communication possible. We try to establish between ourselves and the children a neutral area in which communication is indirect. In other words we participate in shared experiences, about which both we and the children feel something *about something else*, a third thing, which unites us, but which at the same time keeps us safely apart because it does not involve direct exchange between us. Shared experiences are perhaps the only non-threatening form of communication which exists. They can concern almost anything in which we both participate – walks, car rides, playing, drawing, listening to something, looking at something or talking about something. A Child Care Officer found that the only way that she could feel in touch with an unhappy four-year-old was to sit quietly beside him watching his favourite TV programme. This was not a waste of time because the programme brought them together and united them in a way which was tolerable for the child. When this had happened a few times the child was able to sit nearer to the Child Care Officer so that she could quite naturally put her arm round him. Thus was achieved non-verbal communication. If the Child Care Officer had tried to put her arm round the child to begin with, he would have felt threatened and would have resisted.

Shared experiences form invisible links between people which become strengthened as they begin to have a history. Gradually experiences will be referred to and talked over and relived in retrospect, and we shall find that there evolves between us and the child a language for talking in, which is quite special to each child because it contains his or her own words and way of remembering, and imagery, which we take the trouble to learn and to use. If we first take care to learn a child's words and his or her special meaning for things then in time the child will incorporate and use our words and meanings as his or her own.

Once indirect communication has been established by means of shared experiences then there exists an area of life within which direct communication, direct giving and taking, is possible. In fact anything is now possible; the floodgates could be opened or the sparks could fly. Both these events would be signs of life and evidence that real relationships between people, which involve giving and taking, loving and hating, were being established. For instance, the end of the story of the Child Care Officer and the four-year-old boy watching television together was that once having established communication by means of her arm round him, he then on a later occasion was able to throw himself into her arms and cry for his mother who was in hospital. The intensity of his love and longing for his mother was felt in these moments, and this in a sense restored her again for him, and made the mother more real. He could not have reached this point alone. After this event he was noticeably less depressed and unhappy, and began to eat more. On later visits this little boy did not want to cry again, nor did he want the Child Care Officer to put her arm round him again. He wanted to go back to the indirect communication of shared experiences. He brought her his books and his toys and she read and played with him. He certainly looked forward to the Child Care Officer's visits and needed them because he knew that at any time communication of his real feelings to her was possible. And so it is that indirect communication involving a third thing – the shared experience – takes the strain out of life, because it enables people to meet, and at the same time to maintain their separateness, because they feel about something else, not about each other. Within this neutral area no demands are made either way, although at any minute they always *could* be made.

When we have created the conditions for communication between ourselves and the children it is important that we recognize it when it happens, and when they speak to us in the language of feeling we must answer in the same language and not in the language of facts. Feelings are illogical, and it is no good our being logical about them; this simply shows the child that we are not on his wavelength after all. To illustrate what I mean there was the case of a twelve-year-old boy in a Remand Home being visited by a Child Care Officer who had known him before. Towards the end of the interview the boy's father was mentioned and suddenly his eyes filled with tears. The Child Care Officer said: 'Are you worried about your father?' The boy said: 'Yes, I worry about him a lot because his health isn't good and he often seems ill.' The boy looked very distressed and there were more tears. The Child Care Officer said: 'Perhaps you sometimes even feel that your father might die?' The boy said: 'Yes, I do think that, often, and I hate it when he goes out on his bicycle because I always think that he will be brought home dead.' At this point the Child Care Officer lost her nerve and said: 'Well, when I saw your father last week he didn't look at all ill, in fact he was looking very well.' This statement is in the language of facts, and it simply does not reach feeling, and moreover it creates a gulf between the adult and the child. In this case the Child Care Officer might have said something like this: 'I know you are very fond of your father, but perhaps sometimes you feel very angry with him too.' Actually this boy had a great deal about which to be angry with his father, because the father had left the boy's mother, taking the boy away too, and was now living with another woman. At this point the boy started stealing.

So the question of language is an important one, and means that we have to be constantly aware of which language the children are speaking in and to answer them in the same terms, otherwise we shall block communication and leave them frustrated and even more hopeless than ever of being understood.

I now come to the third aspect of my subject and this is to consider why it is that some children present special problems in communication. This matter is of course related to the subject of the social diagnosis in each case. This involves an assessment of the developmental problem with which each child is struggling and the ways in which he is dealing with it. This kind of assessment, which is part of our professional responsibility, is in fact an extension of something which we do automatically in ordinary life. When we meet a child we quite naturally wonder what sort of a child he or she is and what sort of an approach on our part is most likely to meet with a response. In our work, however, we do all this more deliberately and with conscious effort and care because more depends on the success or failure of our efforts and, moreover, if we cannot get on to the wavelength of the individual child we ourselves, as I have suggested, can become the block to communication.

In each case the reason for the difficulty in communication will be a complex one and a highly individual one. The reason will not be an actively deliberate one but will be related to unconscious processes and the drive for self-preservation which is behind all symptoms. The word 'reason' therefore, is a misnomer because it implies conscious thought and choice.

I should like to discuss five kinds of case in which the ability to communicate is seriously impaired or virtually non-existent because the will or drive to communicate is no longer present. These cases will be familiar to all social workers. They are: *the suspicious; the hostile; the withdrawn; the restless extrovert; the depressed.*

1. First, then, there are the children who keep themselves to themselves because they are *suspicious* of anyone or anything outside themselves. The world outside is a bad place and the only way to ensure self-preservation is to have no dealings with the

world. A certain amount of suspicion is of course normal and is part of the natural tendency for self-preservation which is present in us all. Usually, however, we do not remain suspicious – we take the next step, which is to test out the situation or the person to prove if our suspicion is realistic or unfounded, and then we act accordingly. This is happening all the time without our thinking about it. Children are less experienced than adults and therefore have the right to be that much more suspicious. But some people, for a variety of reasons, have lost the courage to test out the situation because they have a deep conviction that their worst fears will come true and they will find that people in the world are as punishing and vindictive as they are feared to be. So they never try to find out, and this at least keeps disaster at bay, although the cost of doing so is high in terms of all that they miss. In many cases suspicion of the world is not a total thing. It becomes fixed on to one thing, e.g. food, or certain places or people or certain activities. This can be difficult to handle, but so long as the suspicions are respected, it does at least give elbow room for development in other directions.

The establishing of communication with a child who is unduly suspicious will obviously take time and patience, because any attempt on our part to break in will only increase suspicion. These children need the opportunity to see us in action so that they can weigh us up and assess our attitudes towards other people and towards themselves, and then one day they may have the courage to test us out in some way or other, when they are ready to do so. I remember seeing a boy of 9, who was a deeply suspicious person, come up to his house-father saying that there was something in his eye. Fortunately the house-father took this very seriously because it was the first time this boy had asked for any personal attention, and although there was actually nothing in his eye, it was bathed and treated with great respect. This was the beginning of a gradual lessening of suspicion. The child communicated, and the communication was received as such. Another example is that of a Child Care Officer who, over a period of many months, had spent much time in the playroom of a children's Home with a suspicious little girl of four years. As soon as the Child Care Officer came into the room this child never took her eyes off her and surreptitiously watched every movement and every contact the Child Care Officer had with any other child, but strongly resisted any move made towards herself. After months of this seemingly futile attempt, the Child Care Officer was one day sitting on the floor talking to another child, when the child in question rolled a ball very slowly across the floor until it touched the Child Care Officer. The Child Care Officer then rolled the ball equally slowly back to the child. The rolling game continued at each visit for a long time and by means of it tension was lessened and communication was gradually expanded.

In the kind of case in which suspicion dominates the scene we know that what is happening can be stated in theoretical terms as the projection by the child of all his or her hostile feelings on to the outside world in an attempt to preserve the goodness within him- or herself.

2. The next kind of case I want to discuss presents the opposite picture. The child himself feels so *angry and hostile* that he fears that he will destroy everyone and everything in sight. Therefore, in order to preserve the outside world, which somehow he at the same time values, he hangs on to his anger and attempts to keep it inside and under control. Such a child will be unable to communicate his real feelings because he fears their destructive potential. When we attempt to get near to him he seems indifferent, passive and unco-operative. These children are often easier to help than the suspicious ones, because deep down they do believe in goodness and are capable of love. First of all, however, we have to meet and survive the hostility and aggression such children truly feel but dare not communicate. We have ample evidence of its existence. Usually it shows on their faces and in their attitude of calculated indifference. Before we can get anywhere this needs facing and putting into words. I am reminded of a probation case in which a twelve-year-old boy remained actively passive for many weeks and obviously found great difficulty in making the slightest response to the Probation Officer. One day the Probation Officer went to collect the boy from the waiting room and on the way out of the room the boy suddenly punched another boy in an angry way. The Probation Officer took him away quickly before a fight started up and said to him: 'You must be pretty mad with someone to hit out like that, and I don't think it's with that boy in the waiting room. I guess you're pretty mad about having to

come here at all and with me for insisting that you do.' The boy admitted that he was angry at having to come and thought it was all a waste of time, etc. As this boy's hostility was met, and recognized, it became possible at last for the two people to meet on a realistic basis. Obviously the boy intended the Probation Officer to see his anger and it was then possible for the Probation Officer to deal with it. But he could not have done so earlier.

3. A third kind of case in which communication in the real sense of the word is very difficult to establish is that of the child whose effective personality is *withdrawn* into him- or herself as a protective measure against dependence and the frustrations and disappointments that go with it. Inadequate personal care and loving attention or the sudden withdrawal of it, or the actual loss of the person depended on, can result in this state of affairs. The child withdraws and so to speak 'looks after' him- or herself. These children do not seem to suffer actively, nor are they overtly hostile or suspicious, because they have put themselves beyond the reach of the ordinary feelings that are part and parcel of all relationships.

Outwardly they comply just enough to maintain their existence with the least effort. We must expect to fail to communicate with many of these children, but that does not mean that we should give up trying and write them off. Perhaps they need our presence in their lives as *the person with whom they do not communicate* and from whom they have withdrawn. This may involve us in silent sessions or in some activity such as reading a story, which makes no demands on them. If we can accept this rôle of the person with whom they do not communicate, without seeking to force our way in, then one day the situation could alter, but if we do not put ourselves in this position and contract out, there is little hope that it will alter. I remember trying to help a young woman in her twenties. She had been a very withdrawn child actually spending most of her time in a large cupboard under the stairs. In here she kept her toys and her possessions, including her radio for listening to 'Childrens' Hour', which she never missed. She only really felt secure when she was in this place. She actually slept in it as well, and as far as possible she kept everyone else, especially her mother, out of it. Many times when I saw her I had to say, because I felt it was true: 'Today you are in your cupboard with all your possessions, and I know that I must not come into it.' Some months later she had a dream that she was in an underground cave—it was warm and cosy—'rather like her cupboard', she said, and there was plenty of food, and I was there and we were going to cook a meal. So there had been an alteration in the situation, and for once I was allowed into the cupboard. But I am sure that this would not have happened if 1 had not accepted the rôle of the person who was *there*, but who was kept outside. In this rather negative way eventually something positive could happen, but what a pity it could not have happened years before.

For some of these withdrawn children maybe only a regression to dependence on the person who is actually living with them and caring for them will bring them through to the place where a real relationship based on the meeting of dependence needs is possible. In other words the place which enables them to give up 'looking after themselves' and be dependent on someone who can then take them forward in the natural way until they can be truly independent within the setting. If this is to happen the person caring for the child will need much support from the Child Care Officer. I have known people who can take children through this kind of experience, but they do not do it easily and need constant reassurance.

4. By contrast with the children who withdraw from the problems of everyday life there are others who may deal with their problems by the opposite kind of reaction which we call a 'flight to reality'. We may regard them as *extrovert*, and find them full of activity, talkative and co-operative. We can easily be misled by these children partly because they are such a relief from the more unresponsible children on our caseload. But in time we notice that their activities change too frequently and they lack sustaining power. They talk too much, and too easily, about anything that comes to mind for comment. What they are doing is clutching at anything that is available outside themselves to prevent themselves from feeling, because feeling would lead to despair and hopelessness. In working with these children we have to beware that we ourselves do not get caught up in their endless merry-go-round that leads nowhere. Here again we have to play a waiting game, establishing ourselves in their lives as someone who can be trusted and with whom they might eventually share their hopelessness.

But they have to make quite sure first that we are not taken in by their excitability. If they could reach with us a moment of true feeling this might enable them to reconstruct their lives on a sounder basis. In other words if they can *feel*, even if it is only to feel the pain of loss and despair, then the way is open for other feelings to come to life again. Many children will not be able to reach this point because it is altogether too painful, and they will construct their lives on an artificial basis. Some may achieve much and be the life and soul of many a party, but they will be inwardly dissatisfied because they are incapable of any real relationship.

5. The last group of children I want to mention as presenting to us problems in communication are those who are obviously in *a depressed state*. They are difficult to reach because they are preoccupied with their own anxieties which may concern their health and bodily functions or their lack of achievements or relationships. Life feels futile because they feel dead inside. We know from experience that any effort we make to encourage these children out of their depression or to distract them or cheer them up, although it may seem to work temporarily is, in the long run, of no avail, because it simply does not reach them. Children in this state cannot believe that anything is good because they doubt their own goodness. They may say, 'Mother is not good', or 'My parents are bad', but even if this is true it is only another way of saying that they themselves are no good. It seems to me that the only way to reach these children is that we ourselves should believe in and acknowledge their feelings of badness and deadness, because they are *real*. We may know that this is not the total truth about them, but at the moment it is. To attempt to cheer them up or get them to snap out of their depression is like a rejection of them, and as such it confirms their feelings about themselves, and removes them still further from us.

If we can 'hold' them as they are in their despair, and understanding is a kind of holding, then there is some chance that they might come to life again. Of course we may find that we do actually hold them physically at times when it seems appropriate. The point is that we cannot bring them to life again in any artificial way by trying to inject them with our belief in their goodness and that life is worth living. Only their own belief will enable them to find it so.

When we fully acknowledge the hopelessness and despair that many children we meet carry around with them, not only is this evidence to them that we are in touch with them, but it means that their feelings are now a stated fact and, as such, are objectified and put outside themselves. This can bring relief and the possibility of an alternative way of living. But if nobody acknowledges the existence of the despairing self the children themselves have to keep it going. It is here that people tend to say that the child is wallowing in despair, but what else can he do with it except to lose touch with feelings?

I have spent some time describing various kinds of case in which we find communication difficult to establish. I am aware that I could add to this list and that I have for instance not mentioned the children who are overtly hostile, but it seems to me that in practice they are not so difficult to communicate with as the cases I have mentioned.

When we feel we are failing to make contact with a particular child, it is only fair to ourselves, let alone to the child concerned, that we should give careful attention to this question of diagnosis, because this affects not only what we do but how much we can reasonably expect to do. We all too easily blame ourselves when we fail to establish communication and feel that our techniques are inadequate (and then we blame those who taught us, or did not teach us) but I suggest that more often than not, it is our assessment that is not adequate.

To sum up I would say that if we believe in the reality of children's feelings we shall not find it difficult to communicate. If on the other hand, we do not have this belief, we cannot get round the difficulty by learning techniques. It is better then to leave alone the subject of communicating with children.

Clare Winnicott first became interested in the problems of children separated from their parents when, after training as a psychiatric social worker, she worked as a welfare officer in the wartime government evacuation scheme. She was then responsible for placing disturbed children in hostels and for working closely with the staff who were caring for them. As a result of the experience gained in this work she was invited to give evidence to the Curtis Committee on the Care of Children. Then for

three years at the end of the war she was a civil liaison officer in a rehabili-
tation unit for ex-prisoners of war, where she was concerned with the
problems of families disrupted as a result of wartime separation. In 1947
she was appointed tutor in charge of a new training course for Child Care
Officers at the London School of Economics, later becoming a lecturer on
the Applied Social Studies Course there. From 1963 to 1971 she was
Director of Child Care Studies with the Central Training Council in Child
Care, being responsible for the organization and oversight of courses of
training for residential staff and for Child Care Officers.

8

The process of symbolization observed among emotionally deprived children in a therapeutic school

The New Era, vol. 44, no. 8, 1963.

B. E. Dockar-Drysdale

This paper carries on the theme of communication with children. Mrs Dockar-Drysdale shares with us her understanding and use of symbolic communication. Those of us who as children have had deeply rewarding shared family experiences may recall family traditions, sayings or rituals which symbolize the warmth and richness of the experience. Children who have no available store of such family memories to draw upon, use moments of symbolic communication with a residential worker or therapist to fill this gap in their lives. The sharing of the process of symbolization needs a delicate awareness and sensitivity from the child care worker, and Mrs Dockar-Drysdale demonstrates how this both can lead to a deeper understanding of the child on the part of the worker and also provides a real positive store of therapeutic experience which can be drawn upon later if needed.

My aim in this paper is to isolate one particular process, 'Symbolization', from the many complicated processes through which children are moving on their journey to integration as individuals. In our therapeutic school for disturbed children, we have come to speak of the particular group whom we are trying to help as emotionally deprived, (rather than simply maladjusted or disturbed) in as much that these are children who have had gaps in the continuity of their existence at the beginning of their lives.

We are thinking in terms of a series of processes which must be gone through in order to reach integration. These are experience, realization, symbolization and conceptualization. By this I mean quite simply that a child may have a good experience provided by his therapist, but that this will be of no value to him until he is able, eventually, to realize it; that is to say to feel that this good thing has really happened to him. Then he must find a way of storing the good thing inside him, which he does by means of symbolizing the experience. Last in the series of processes comes conceptualization, which is understanding intellectually what has happened to him in the course of the experience, and being able to think this in words: conceptualization is only of value if it is retrospective–ideas must be the sequel to experience. There are many people who have had to substitute ideas for experience, who then try to force subsequent experience into the Procrustean bed of an organized system of ideas. Even coming straight on the heels of emotional experience, conceptualization is premature and arid. These other processes, realization and symbolization, provide the essential stepping stones to what, after all, conceptualization really is, an economic method of storing experience, and at the same time establishing the means of communicating experience. It is not enough to give emotionally deprived children good experience, we must also help them to keep the good things inside them, or they will lose them once more.

Babies who have 'good enough' mothers are able to proceed at their own pace from experience to conceptualization. The emotionally deprived children who come to us for treatment have not had 'good enough' mothering. The first year of their lives has been interrupted by disaster, there are gaps which have never been filled, and they lack the necessary experience for which to need storage space. They are not, of course, aware of this–'you do not miss what you have never had'–but when children have had primary provision of the kind I have described, they achieve realization, and frequently express their difficulty in finding storage in their minds for their new experiences.

In the Mulberry Bush School, where I work as Therapeutic Adviser, we attempt to evolve a therapy of provision; we try in a therapeutic milieu to fill these gaps at the beginning of such children's lives. In this paper, however, I shall not be talking so much about the nature of the therapeutic provision which we make for the children at the Bush, as about the means they use to store what we provide, through the use of symbols.

David said to me, 'I haven't room inside me to keep the memory of all the things that have happened to me here.'

Maurice said (showing me a procession of animals, wild and tame, at the beginning of a book of fairy tales), 'How can I have wild lions and tame cows inside together?' (His love and his hate.)

Sefton said, 'I need a box inside me to keep things in that have happened.'

Robert said, 'I can't keep all the words about all the things inside my mind, there just isn't room, no one could remember all that. There must be another way of keeping what I remember.' The 'other way' to which he referred is symbolization.

Now and then a very disturbed child may be referred to us who has integrated in some areas, and has been able to contain, realize and symbolize some emotional experience, even though this has been traumatic.

Robert in his first session with me drew (from a squiggle) a staircase. Half-way up the stairs there was a gigantic step. When asked 'How could anyone climb that step?' he replied, 'I couldn't – it was too big – what can I do?' I suggested (trying to communicate with him in his own symbolic language) that he might be able to build a small ladder, which would enable him to go on up the stairs, but that I thought nothing could be done to alter the step. He accepted this proposal and asked me to help him to build the ladder. Here was someone who had a traumatic gap in his experience, who had realized this, and had symbolized the experience, and contained the symbols in a form which could be communicated. Had I asked him, 'What do you think went wrong when you were little?' he could not have told me. Actually, Robert was very small when his brother was born, and his young and inadequate mother felt quite unable to look after two babies at once – so she gave the new baby all the primary experience at her disposal, at the same time cutting off adaptation to Robert's needs and depriving him of the final stages of integration. This was the 'gap' – this was the gigantic step in the staircase which he could not climb; but he was able to tell me about his problem because of his capacity for symbolization.

Recently I met Jacqueline for the first time. She was most unwilling to have anything to do with me, hid behind the chair, covered her face with her hands, and in various ways mimed hiding from me. Presently, however, we found that she would like me 'to call her on the toy telephone'. I asked, when at last I got the right number!—from where she was ringing, and she said 'Behind the tree in my garden!' The telephone conversation continued, and Jacqueline gradually started to talk about herself in a way which I felt she might regret later, because I was sure she was not intending consciously to trust me with such information. So I said, 'It sounds to me as though you are coming out from behind the tree in your garden.' Jacqueline was furious and screamed, 'You shouldn't have said that—now I'll go right over the garden wall.' I said that she was quite right to go over the wall, but if she came back into the garden I would know she wanted to do this, and was not just coming by mistake. Presently we re-established our discussion on this new basis. Here again this child, who was very mistrustful of me, was able to convey her attitudes, and to open a field of communication with me. She could certainly not have had the conscious insight to conceptualize these attitudes, to understand the complex cross-currents of feeling which she was experiencing. Nevertheless, she *realized what she was feeling symbolized* her fear of me and was, therefore, in a position to *tell me* about her panic reaction to my words.

Sometimes one sees very clearly that a child may be driven to acting out in the environment because he has been unable to symbolize, so that acting out *in a symbolic way* becomes the only means of communication apparently available to him. This is a very common reason for the wild outbursts of destructive and aggressive behaviour which one associates with disturbed children.

Porky had been slowly approaching complete integration as the result of the continuous care of his therapist (Vanno Weston). The crisis occurred when two newcomers were introduced into Vanno's group, an event which all too faithfully reproduced the birth of the next babies in Porky's family. He broke down into chaotic and destructive behaviour, doing everything he could to produce a state of stress so acute that Vanno would refuse to keep him in her group. (In the original disastrous situation he had been sent to a children's home for a period.) It was possible for Vanno and myself to make Porky see what he was doing unconsciously, and I told him that he might find it possible to help Vanno to look after the new members of the group, which he had never been able to do in the original context with his mother and the babies. (Vanno has asked him to help her to look after a bowl of bulbs for her, which will be a symbolic means of identification with her in caring for new life.) Porky broke down into a frenzy of acting out through a failure to symbolize traumatic experience in the original situation, and a subsequent inability to communicate his suffering in any socially acceptable form, in a context which felt to him like the original trauma.

Perhaps this is the place to try to say something about 'sublimation', and to compare this concept with symbolization. I think it might be true to say that symbolization is the first step *towards* sublimation; but that symbolization is a much easier and more primitive mechanism. Symbolization can be used, as we have seen, in plenty of ways, but I think the aim of symbolization remains constant—that is *to store a realized experience in such a way that this can be preserved and, if need be, communicated*. Remember, however, that all the early important experiences happen in the baby's life *before he can speak*.

I have spoken elsewhere about adaptation to individual needs, and the kind of symbolic adaptation which turns up in the provision of primary experience also aims at giving the child localized experience in a symbolic form, which can be stored by him. The form the therapist uses for such an adaptation must be acceptable to the child, but nevertheless when he subsequently *realizes* the experience he has been given through the adaptation, he may make use of other symbols in order to store this experience. One could say quite simply that symbolization is a way of keeping things which could not be kept in any other way.

Sublimation, however, is a more mature process, involving change of *aim*. There must be a really integrated person present for sublimation to be a relevant concept, a person capable of making identifications. Such a person will have had experience, realized, symbolized and conceptualized, and will have gone on to identify with important people in his life (his parents, or parent figures) and to have aims other than relieving instinctual tensions. He is now able to make use of instinctual drives, harness them, and redirect them to help him to achieve his aims. What often happens of course is that people 'displace' (aggression for example), but displacement does *not* imply a change of aim.

Let us go back to Porky and the bulbs. Vanno, you will remember, is going to ask Porky to help her *to look after a bowl of bulbs*. You can see how different this will be from a situation in which Vanno might *give* Porky a bowl of bulbs, or where Porky might attack Vanno's bowl of bulbs (perhaps pull them up and destroy them). I want you to think of these three possibilities in terms of Porky's present and original problem. There were the babies his mother bore after him, and in the same way the new children whom Vanno has accepted recently into her group. (Of course, a bowl of bulbs could be used in quite a different way in another emotional context.) Traumatic experience which has not been internalized, realized and so on, will be likely to be repeated: that is to say, the child will always be meeting situations which will feel the same as the original trauma. Our aim in treatment is to help him to deal effectively with such traumatic re-experiences, and to complete them in a creative way.

If Vanno were to give Porky the bowl of bulbs she would be saying, in a symbolic way, that Porky could be the father of the family represented by the bowl, herself, (the mother figure) and the bulbs (the babies). This would be by-passing the current problem, and facing Porky with an even more difficult dilemma— that of having been allowed to steal the father's rights, in other words Vanno would be in collusion with Porky in obtaining, albeit symbolically, satisfaction to which he would have no right. She would be putting herself in a false position. If Porky were to destroy Vanno's bowl of bulbs he would be displacing his rage against Vanno and the babies—the new children. It would obviously be better for the bulbs to be destroyed than for Vanno and the children to be hurt, but there would be no change of Porky's aim, which would remain destructive. However, by asking Porky *to help her to look after the bulbs in the bowl*, she is enabling the child to symbolize his realization that although he is no longer 'the only baby' or 'the newest baby', nor the father of the family and, therefore, Vanno's husband, nevertheless he has his own place in the group-family, and can identify with Vanno's care of the new ones because she has helped him to find symbols, and to use them in a way which will help him, so that his experiences can become creative and growing rather than traumatic and interrupting growth as they were originally. The cruelty which he might have shown towards the children or the bulbs, can now, through his understanding of Vanno's feelings, become changed into pity and a wish to protect the young and helpless, in just the way that toddlers are helped to change their cruel feelings towards the new babies into compassion and care because their mother enlists their help, making it possible for them to identify with her aims, so different from those of the toddlers.

There is a tremendous amount more to be said about sublimation, but at least one can see from Porky's treatment situation that one can symbolize, or duplicate in a symbolic way, without sublimation taking place–that it matters therefore, very much how one uses symbols.

The next child I want to talk about is David. He is of good average intelligence and is nine and a half years old. Recently he came to see me and found me writing the beginning of this paper. He asked me questions about what I was writing, and when I had answered him, remarked that he would like to write something of the sort himself–about the work being done for children at the Bush. For various reasons which we consider later, I suggested that if he could do this I would be prepared to have his 'essay' typed inside my own and read it with mine. I only wish to make one comment before I give you his essay, which is that this child has only survived emotionally through his ability *to conceptualize immediately following experience*. He is a boy 'full of ideas' as you will see: he makes, however, no use of symbols, and until recently he intellectualized everything, to the exclusion of feeling and realization. Whenever feeling broke through this intellectual defence he panicked. He has recently been through deep primary and 'gap filling' experiences at the Bush, and some of these have been in key sessions alone with me, although many others have been with Mildred Levious, who looks after his group. I have been the Supporter in this case, but have been used more directly than usual by the child.

ESSAY ABOUT THE BUSH—BY DAVID

People have come to understand things at the Bush, that need help. And, some people found it difficult without the Bush. And sometimes they find it difficult to understand about it. And it is more easier to understand in the country. Sometimes they need help because their mothers died when they were little babies and sometimes they found it difficult to learn at other schools—like me over sums what I found difficult. And sometimes they've come to the Bush so that they can start their things all over again so they can remember.

And when they leave the Bush they may find it easier when they are learning at other schools, and sometimes they've come because they've got into a lot of muddles, and so that they can get the muddle undone; like getting knitting that's muddled undone, but it is a bit more complicated than undoing wool, isn't it? But when they first come here they find it quite panicky, but when they have been here a while they find it all right, like I did.

And the staff try to help to get things better and some staff find it difficult, that's students like D. . . ., but she wanted to do the same sort of jobs but she found it difficult.

Sometimes the children find the staff difficult, like when they won't do what they want. Sometimes their mum and dad find it difficult to keep them and look after them. We come to Mrs D. to talk about things, and then we find it more easier to understand.

Sometimes they find it frightening at the Bush, and then they get used to it. It's important this—they come to understand about things that go wrong with them at the Bush, and then they get an easier life wherever they go.

But some children find it hard to understand. And when they are at the Bush they find it easier to come to understand about their own lives, isn't that true?—really this is a lot of knowledge isn't it?

Some people go to homes and find the difficulty more complicated, what I mean by that is that the home makes it even more difficult, and they have to go to another home.

Grown-ups come and see first whether they can manage this work, because they have to understand everything about helping children, all that they have to know about that goes on.

People that leave the Bush who found it too hard, find the work they can do—the kind they like best. When they stay it means they've found the sort of work they can do best, and they do all sorts of things to help the children, so that when they leave they find it more easier to get on with other people.

Sometimes grown-ups think of plans that they can do (like having sum cards so that children can get on with their work). At the Bush they can let you start all over again in all sorts of ways. In other schools they wouldn't.

The Bush stops you when you're growing up not knowing all about complicated things from grown-ups not understanding. I'm making up—thinking about the things I really know. This kind of work may need to go on for a long time because when muddled children have children *they* may need this work to be done for them.

I got left behind, and now I'd learn and not get left behind. Because the easier you find things the less panics, and you're not feeling sad all the time, cos then you can't do things and learn all that. But when you are grown up you don't feel so sad because you know your mother can't live for ever and ever, but when you're a child it's different, and you haven't had your life. But when I get old my life will end, it'll be all a life, that's the sort of thing you need to understand.

It doesn't take very long these days to help people, like it used to be, cos these days people are a bit more clever and have learnt more. [*Aside:* DAVID: Why does if feel warmer in your room than in any other room? MYSELF: Is it, perhaps, just because you feel safe in it?]

In the old days they didn't need much help, they didn't have to think so much because they had not learnt so much, so things were not so complicated.

Now people don't have to work so hard, they have stoves instead of fires. In the olden days if a tooth came out they didn't go to a dentist because there wasn't one. They were too busy to be so worried.

They didn't live so long or have so much money, so things are easier now: but people find it a hard world and get into a lot of muddles because everything is so fast. In those days you see people couldn't get run over because there wasn't any cars! (That's a sort of a joke.)

Sometimes people find it hard to keep children because they have to work—that's why children have to go to homes. I mean the parents get into difficulties with their children, and the fathers find it hard to cope with the mothers, and the mothers with the fathers, and the children sometimes find it easier to be somewhere else. [*Aside:* DAVID: Poochie is getting much bigger, isn't she? MYSELF: I think you know that Poochie is going to have puppies soon.]

Some people just think about it, some people talk about it and get all the feelings over, that's why talking in talks about feelings makes them understand more.

My essay is different from Mrs D.'s, and it is the same way about the Bush except that some other people don't think the same thing, do they? It didn't take me long to understand, but it takes other people longer sometimes because they have reasons that make it more difficult to understand. And children at the Bush are not easy to live with, are they?

This is an important thing (my essay being inside Mrs. D.'s) because when you are inside an essay it's more complicated than being inside your mother.

It isn't all that different because it's about the same home–or school. People should really have their own essays about their life.

When you are first a little baby it isn't so hard for your mother to look after you, but as you get bigger it gets difficulter, and the more people you have the harder it would be, and that's an important reason for schools like the Bush, and that means when you've been here and grown older it's easier for your mum to look after you.

There are many interesting points in David's essay, but what I want you to notice especially is the fact that although the essay is essentially a work of ideas, of rather surprisingly definite conceptualization, nevertheless, without this ever having been stated, David feels that for his little essay to be inside my big one is comparable to a baby being in its mother. This was what I hoped he would feel, and the two asides show how aware he was becoming of his symbolic experience before he made the statement, '. . . when you are inside an essay it is more complicated than being inside your mother.' The asides showing his growing awareness of what this experience was meaning to him were, you may remember . . .

'D. Why does it feel warmer in your room than in any other room?

MYSELF: Is it perhaps just because you feel safe in it?'
And

'D. Poochie is getting much bigger, isn't she?

MYSELF: I think you know that Poochie is going to have puppies soon.'

What I was trying to do (and this attempt was successful, as it happened) was to show David that he could actually have symbolic experience with me which could feel real, that he could realize this and store the experience. The experience I offered him had to do with his ideas but, nevertheless, helped him towards symbolization. He had told me that he would never be able to be inside his mother again, any more than he could be inside me, because this would be practically impossible, but here he was being able to find out for himself that in a symbolic way this could be done, and could feel real to him. Of course I had made no interpretation to him. Had I said, 'Perhaps to have your essay inside mine would feel like being a baby again inside your mother,' I would have made it impossible for him to have the experience; he would just have had another idea for his Encyclopedia, as it were.

Sechehaye calls this 'symbolic realization', and my impression is that when this kind of thing happens the process is symbolic experience followed by realization.

David's essay is full of insight and is especially valuable because less than a year ago David was a very ill child, who behaved as though he were mad. Both his parents are deeply troubled people. David said earlier, 'My mum is always getting into a muddle and so am I.' These 'muddles' were terrible panics which overwhelmed him every few minutes, and made him violent and destructive. Recently he stated 'I don't get into muddles any more, though I sometimes have a muddle in me—but that's different.' Of course David might not have used the material offered him—had he not done so I would have assumed that I was wrong in supposing that he could use these particular symbols to record his experience of having felt contained by me in the treatment situation. As it was he now had a means of storing both the therapeutic experiences with me, and the original experience with his mother, which he knew about intellectually without having reached realization or symbolization. I could, however, only offer him the symbols, it was for David to decide whether he would make use of them.

Michael was just about to settle down for the night, when he suddenly asked me, 'Can you give me something to take into my sleep with me?' I had absolutely nothing appropriate with me, yet I was so sure that he really needed *something*, and that he would know how 'to take it into his sleep with him', that I felt in my coat pocket and found a minute gold safety pin, which I handed to him in a matter of fact sort of way, before saying 'goodnight'.

He accepted the little safety pin, and in the morning came to tell me about a dream—the first dream he could remember.

'I dreamt', he said, 'that I was walking along a road. There was a baby with its nappy undone, and it was crying: so I pinned up the nappy with my little gold pin and the baby was all right.

I went on down the road and I met a boy whose braces had broken, so that his trousers were coming down, so I fixed his braces with my little gold pin and the boy was all right.

I went on down the road and I met a man. The wind was blowing cold and the top button had come off his coat, so I gave him my little gold pin to fasten it, and the man was all right.'

This was a very important first dream, but all I want to say here is that children can make use of symbols in an astonishing way. I think you will be well aware from what I have said that one of the most important and difficult tasks in working with deeply disturbed children, is to establish such means of communication as I have described—so often they have kept some small but precious store of symbols representing their earliest experiences, but there has been nobody to whom they felt that they could communicate.

Johnnie, aged seven, whom I met for the first time yesterday, said, 'I am going to sing you a song that has been inside me for a long time.' Here is

JOHNNIE'S SONG

The little boat sails
On the water
And the little boat sails
On the waves.
And the little boat did
And the waves was dead.
Then the waves had nothing
To do with the little boat.
There was nothing for the little boat.

Johnnie's song referred to his babyhood. He talked presently to me about the storm which had caused the waves which tossed the little boat about, until even they were dead and there was nothing left. What we reached later in the session was that there was a time when the little boat was rocking gently on the still and sunlit sea—the time before the storm. As Johnnie said, 'I did not know there was a beginning to the song, it is like there being an o before there is 1.'

I think all of us have unsung songs; unpainted pictures; unwritten pieces of music inside us—the artists, and the poets, and the musicians can communicate these in such a way that they sing, paint, or play their earliest experiences, and find a response in us because we have also had a golden age at the beginning of our lives. But the disturbed children whom we try to help in our school, all too often have no unsung song within them. They have had nothing about which to sing.

SUMMARY

Symbolization is a necessary process for the internalization and preservation of experience at the beginning of life. I have said very little about the origins of the symbols themselves. On what are symbols based? I think we can only suppose that they have their origins in the earliest bodily experiences, and that it is the realization and symbolization of these which provides the prototype for this important process.

In working with emotionally deprived children who have gaps in their primary experience, it becomes essential—having provided missing experience in a way which feels real to the child—that we should help him to realize and symbolize these experiences, so that they can become part of himself and he can reach ideas about the experiences. Such provision of missing experience is often in itself symbolic, but will need to be realized and symbolized all the same if it is to be of value. Children who have succeeded in symbolizing some areas at least of their earliest experience can communicate this to us; it is essential that we should be able to receive and respond to such communications. Children who are able to communicate in this symbolic way, will be able to tell us all sorts of 'inside' things about themselves, and their own inner worlds, which would otherwise not be reached.

Lastly, conceptualization is no substitute for original experience. This is a process of emotional evolution of individual personality, not an organization of fixed ideas about child rearing.

A biographical note for Mrs Dockar-Drysdale appears on pages 63–64.

9

Observations on runaway children from a residential setting

Child Welfare, vol. 42, no. 6, June 1963.

Donald S. Farrington, William Shelton and James R. MacKay

In America as in this country, children who run away from Homes or schools cause staff to worry. Apart from our natural anxiety about how the child will fare on its own, running away feels to us like rejecting the good care we want to give. The authors of this article describe a number of different reasons which may cause such behaviour. Often running away may be a response to an emotional crisis, which may reactivate anxieties related to a child's own family situation, so that children run away to avoid an imagined danger or in an attempt to solve problems in their home; some inadequate children appear to drift away in an aimless manner and the authors suggest that such children might be helped by a more controlled environment. In this country most residential staff are not in a position to choose the children to be placed with them, but an analysis of the reasons for a child to run away can lead to a deeper understanding of a child's feelings and so become a step in his progress towards stability.

Some children at residential treatment centres express their problems by running away. Although this is recognized as a symptom of emotional disturbance, it is particularly difficult for the staff to cope with, because it implies failure for them and real danger to the child. If children are to be helped in their total personality development, however, the causes of this symptom, like all others, must be understood and appropriate treatment must be offered. To help bring about a treatment orientation in regard to runaways, twenty-eight children at the Spaulding Youth Centre were studied. These youngsters had absented themselves without permission on a combined total of eighty-five occasions for periods of time ranging from several hours to nineteen days. This report presents our clinical observations on the causes of the runaways and their effect on the children and staff. We will also make some recommendations for methods of treatment and management of such children.

Reporting on runaway children in 1956, Paull found that, 'Examination of the literature reveals surprisingly little on this subject, so that no bibliography is attempted. . . .'[1] Although one retrospective study was published[2] and the authors know of another completed study,[3] a review of the literature since 1956 reveals a continued dearth of publications concerning runaway children. One of the objectives of this report is to fill this void in the literature.

The Spaulding Youth Centre is an open institution devoted to the care and treatment of emotionally disturbed children. Located in central New Hampshire it is within walking distance of Tilton, where the children attend school. The majority of the children are placed at the centre by their parents or by social agencies. Since every child is seen in weekly psychotherapeutic interviews, extensive information was available on all the children studied. We knew not only their backgrounds and personalities, but also their daily adjustment within the cottage and at school. Every child who had run away was interviewed by a member of the staff as soon as possible after being apprehended. The interviews took place under a variety of conditions, at all hours, and in such widely divergent settings as a church and a police station.

The average age of the twenty-eight children, twenty-two boys and six girls, when they were admitted to the centre was 13.5 years. They had absented themselves from one to seventeen times,

---

[1] Joseph E. Paull, 'The runaway foster child', *Child Welfare*, vol. 35, no. 7 (1965), 21.

[2] Lee N. Robins, Ph.D. and Patricia O'Neal, M.D., 'The Adult Prognosis for Runaway Children', *American Journal of Orthopsychiatry*, vol. 29 (1959), 752–61.

[3] Robert M. Counts, M.D., *et al.*, 'Running away as an attempted solution to a family problem', unpublished paper (Worcester, Mass.: Worcester Youth Guidance Centre, 1961).

usually for about one day, with an average of three runaways each. Beyond this, we will not attempt to make a statistical presentation. Rather, our observations are impressionistic, although based on considerable clinical experience.

Our observations clearly establish that there is no single causal factor to explain the runaway behaviour of this group of children. What did emerge, however, was a number of constructs, somewhat dissimilar in nature, which we will illustrate and discuss.

During the first week of Bill's residence at the centre he was reported as missing. After some searching, Bill was discovered at 3 a.m. curled up asleep inside a clothes dryer at the local all-night laundry. He was obviously frightened and was initially non-communicative.

It was decided to explore the circumstances immediately, so Bill and his social worker went to an all-night restaurant to talk. Bill said that the boys in his cottage had 'initiated' him, but he was loathe to talk about it further. After more discussion, however, Bill revealed that one of the boys had taken him aside and attempted to force him into a homosexual act. This precipitated a panic, during which Bill fled the cottage.

The social worker then dealt with two aspects of the situation: first, to uncover and discuss the precipitating factors and, second, to help the boy regain his homeostatic balance. The information gained was then used to better understand the boy in the long-term casework interviews.

Several months have passed since this event, and Bill has not run away again. By turning this incident into a therapeutically valuable experience, the casework relationship had been advanced considerably for a boy who had presented a most difficult therapeutic challenge. Bill's family background was marked by social disorganization and deprivation—sickness, emotional disturbance, epilepsy, irresponsibility, divorce, violence, suicide, and homicide. His father was described as 'mean and cruel, a man who never supported the family well and frequently beat up the mother'. His son has not seen him for over ten years. Bill's maternal grandfather had many of the characteristics of his father. He was described as 'cruel, unfaithful, and a heavy drinker, who often beat up family members'.

He was murdered at fifty-three. There was constant friction between Bill and his mother, including threats by Bill and a serious attack on his mother, during which he tried to strangle her. It appears that he was placed in much the same rôle as his grandfather and father had filled.

The residential staff found it easy to understand the underlying mechanism involved in Bill's running away. A sudden crisis–the homosexual advance–had occurred in his life, which led him into a severe panic reaction and flight. His flight was aimless and his only motivation was to get away from the situation as quickly as possible. It has been our experience that such episodes, when understood and dealt with psychotherapeutically, will not be repeated. Bill is continuing with the programme at the centre and is making progress.

Joe was absent from the cottage on a bitterly cold day. Footprints in the snow led to the edge of the nearby river. After anxious hours, it was found that he had carefully backtracked over his own footprints and had hidden in the barn, where he could hear all the efforts being made to locate his body in the river. Finally, he casually walked back into the cottage as if nothing had happened.

One of eleven children, Joe had a history of destructive, aggressive behaviour against his siblings and in his home. Recognizing unconsciously that at the centre runaways were as quick a way of mobilizing the attention of the important adults as destructiveness was at home, Joe chose this method of focusing attention on himself.

Joe represents a second group of children who were runaways in so far as they were absent from their places in the centre. Although the staff did not know their whereabouts, the children were usually on the institution grounds, having used the 'runaway' as an attention-getting device.

'The guys are picking on me. That's why I ran away. In the TV room, Sunday night, they picked on me. Bill said he'd punch my nose if I stayed in the room and Fred said he'd punch me if I left. If I sat down, someone would pull the chair out from under me. The kids here don't like me.' This was Sam's explanation for his running away, one of three runs during his stay at the centre. When Sam was placed with boys his age, he was confused and bewildered by their aggression and unable to cope with their teasing. Basically, Sam hoped to maintain the *status quo*. He had few interests, found it hard to make friends, and tended to be withdrawn; he rarely got himself involved in competitive situations. When a particular situation became unbearable to Sam, he had a simple prescription: to get away from what was bothering him.

Sam had been placed in an institution when he was two years old. He had never known a consistent family and had lived in a series of orphanages and foster homes. His mother was borderline intellectually and his father deserted the family when Sam was born. In the last two foster homes, where there was a good deal of confusion, Sam eventually ran away with no particular goal in mind except the vague hope that he would find his father, whom he had never seen. Basically Sam was quite inadequate, had borderline intellectual ability, and little interest in life. He was rarely troubled by anxiety or concern, and his basic reaction to stress was withdrawal.

Sam is representative of a group of children who are inadequate personalities—borderline intellectually and in other ways—and who find it most difficult to adjust in the residential centre. They may be said to drift away rather than run away. Their somewhat aimless retreat is a manifestation of their need for protection and succour.

Joan, who stayed at the centre for sixteen months, ran away six weeks after she came and again on ten other occasions. The circumstances surrounding the running were consistent—it was usually preceded by a period of depression, nightmares, strong ambivalent feelings toward her mother, and quite often, many somatic complaints. Her absences were for short periods of time, a few hours or overnight, and they were always in opposition to specific rules of the centre. Most often, she would run away to meet a boy, and on a couple of occasions, had sexual intercourse. On her return, she told of what happened, obviously anticipating punishment and removal from the centre.

She had come to the centre following a severe crisis at home. She and her mother had been in conflict about the suitability of Joan's companions, and when Joan once stayed out all night, she was met on her return by her mother's threat to beat her. Therefore, she ran away – she lived outdoors for ten days, sleeping in barns and abandoned cars, eating berries, grass, and food that her friends brought her. When she took the clothing she needed from clothes-lines, she was brought to the attention of the court.

Joan's relationship with her mother and her mother's personality appear to have a direct relationship to her runaway behaviour. Her mother, a withdrawn, frightened woman, had many serious phobias concerning death and disease. Her fear of doctors, however, was equal to her fear of illness. She was openly concerned that Joan would become sexually involved with boys – on one occasion she had barricaded the home so that Joan could not go out. Joan's absences and her behaviour during them appeared to be exactly what her mother both feared and wanted.

The group that Joan represents is both the largest and the most complex. In these cases, the running appears to be directly related to the children's past and present relationships with their families. Perhaps the key to understanding this group's behaviour is the linkage between past home experiences and present milieu experiences in the residential centre. This interrelationship is seen in a variety of ways. For instance, previous studies have demonstrated that some children attempt to resolve an intense family problem by running away. Counts, *et al.*, reported their impressions on a group of girls who had run away from home:

'Strong forces within the parents and the girl lead in the direction of intense acting out within the home usually of a sexual nature. In most instances, overt acting out of the oedipal (or other) themes does not occur. In exceptional situations . . . it may occur. At one point however, the possibility of acting out within the home seems too dangerous, and the girl runs to avoid such an occurrence. She runs to avoid both the internal and external pressures encouraging sexual acting out. The parents, in addition to the girl, want to defend against such a possibility. It is as though her leaving is a relief to all participants. Often they have subtly opened the door and said in effect; "You can solve this dilemma by leaving." In some such cases the parents have even, before the running away made remarks, such as, "You better hadn't run away." At other times it has not been so precise.'[1]

If, in the residential setting, the child finds himself again 'in the middle' of a similar relationship among cottage parents, there will be a repetition of the earlier runaways. The concept of repetition compulsion seems to apply in these situations. The child may raise the cottage parent's anxiety level further by advising him of his intention to run away, saying, 'You'll miss me when I'm gone,' and implying that the cottage parent will be the guilty one for forcing a runaway.

Occasionally, incidents within the institutional setting contribute to precipitating a runaway. For instance, a child's inability to handle feelings of loss, whether real or imagined, can be the triggering factor.

Ralph's father was arrested and sentenced to prison, and his mother was hospitalized and dying. When he went to his therapist to discuss the situation, he was told that his therapist was leaving the agency to continue his studies. Ralph ran away to a large city and got a job. He was returned to the agency after several days.

Another expression of the relationship between running away from the centre and the family is the returning home of a child who fears that 'something is wrong at home' or 'my family needs me at home' or that one or the other parent at home may be ill. The child feels severe anxiety although he may recognize that there is nothing specific to verify his fear. Occasionally, this follows a recent family visit or a letter, but it can also occur after a prolonged period of no communication with the family.

This kind of concern seems to have at least two roots: first, the memory of repeated family crises involving parental illness or separation from a parent because of court action, temporary

[1] *Ibid.*, p. 7.

desertion, or other social action, and second, strong unconscious (sometimes even conscious) hostile feelings toward their parents. The anxiety appears to be based partly on the expectation that their unconscious wishes involving the death, harm or banishment of their parents will be fulfilled. As this anxiety develops, they react by running away to their families to reassure themselves about conditions at home; usually, they are quite willing to return to the residential setting after this.

Another manifestation of this phenomenon is often a source of great concern to cottage parents. Unexpectedly, the cottage parent becomes the object of a great deal of hostility and ridicule. A previously agreeable child may become a serious management problem. Also, the cottage parent may find that he is being compared to the child's parents in an unfavourable light. Eventually, the child runs to a home that, in his absence, he has idealized, only to find the home situation substantially unchanged. Two psychological mechanisms have been brought into play: (1) the simple defence mechanisms of denying all problems at home and (2) a reversal in which the cottage parents become the bad parents and the natural parents are idealized.

Somewhat akin to the preceding group are the children who become involved in a never-ending search for lost parents. One boy, returning from an abortive runaway attempt, explained, 'I was planning to see my uncle in California.' He had not seen his uncle for more than eight years, but recalled the short period of time when his uncle cared for him. Another youngster, born out of wedlock and not knowing who his father was, made the following comment when he was returned after having run away: 'You aren't going to believe this, but I met my real father when I was walking down the street.'

In recent years, there has been general agreement that all members of a residential treatment staff must be involved in the rehabilitation programme if it is to be truly effective. An attempt was made to use this concept to understand and manage the problem of runaways.

Like most residential centres, the Spaulding Youth Centre has a preplacement visit for those children applying for admission. It is during this period that the staff has the opportunity to observe the child's behaviour, read the historical material from the referring agency, administer psychological tests, and conduct diagnostic interviews. Based on this accumulation of data, the staff makes a decision about the child's ability to make use of the programme. If the child is accepted, they develop a total treatment programme for him from this material. This is the best time to refuse acceptance to those children who cannot benefit from the programme because of their propensity for running away. Those children who come within the third category described above–withdrawing children with inadequate personalities–generally need an institutional placement different from that provided by a residential treatment centre. Although the staff may be swayed by the children's obvious need for help, it can best be found in a more protected setting.

For those children who have attempted to deal with problems at home by running away, there is every likelihood that they will repeat this behaviour in the residential setting. This does not mean, however, that the child cannot make use of the programme. Rather, it means that careful exploration must be made in this area. Our experience shows that the large majority of these children can be helped in the residential setting and that the runaway behaviour can be used therapeutically to help the child clarify his relationship with his family.

In general, the intake process attempts to limit admission to children who can be maintained in a residential programme, who are not chronic runaways, or whose running away could be therapeutically utilized and would not eventuate in further harm for the child.

Once the decision is made to accept a child who is or may become a runaway problem, it is crucial that his behaviour be understood and incorporated into the initial planning of his programme. At this point, all staff members are involved in understanding the child and in planning for his stay at the residential centre. Staff is involved at two levels–formal and informal. On a formal level, frequent meetings are held for all staff, at which they present cases and are encouraged to discuss them. Ordinarily, the therapist to whom the child is assigned presents the facts and the staff psychiatrist presides over the meeting and leads the discussion, which involves all levels of staff–cottage parents; teachers;

athletic, medical, and clinical staff; and others, Occasionally, it is interesting to present subjects of special interest, such as an explanation of runaway behaviour, in these conferences. It is most useful, however, if these presentations are tied to areas of current concern.

Less formal than these organized staff meetings is the consultant relationship that the child's therapist forms with other staff members. The therapist therefore has two specific responsibilities. The formal one-to-one therapeutic relationship and the group-therapy relationship with a child are well understood and require no elaboration. The responsibility the therapist has as a consultant to other staff members is less well understood, however. This technique although utilized in a less formal manner than staff meetings and scheduled individual conferences, should be used consciously by the social worker.

Crisis situations such as the one facing Bill provide a good opportunity for consultation with the staff in the interest of the child. The staff experiences feelings of guilt, concern, and anger when they try to deal with the child's absence and eventual return. The social worker in this instance is aware not only of the child's reason for running away but also of the effect it will have on the staff, of what part staff members think they played in the runaway, and of the part they actually did play. Such an understanding can help prevent further disruption for the child on his return. In discussing these interrelationships with a staff member, the social worker should use the child's behaviour as the focal point for discussion since the feeling of a staff member can be best dealt with that way. For example, it may be helpful for a cottage parent to be aware that a child has had a long history of running away that is related to conflict within his family, If he understands that these children do tend to repeat this kind of behaviour, he can see that the minor argument he had with his wife just before the child ran away did not cause the runaway, although it may have served as the trigger. In this way, the cottage parent is relieved of unnecessary guilt and has a new understanding of the child that can be useful in the future.

Staff understanding of the dynamics of runaway behaviour has been used to prevent these absences, the consequent severe disruptions for the child and staff, and the real dangers involved.

Within the therapeutic relationship, the therapist has the opportunity to deal directly with the underlying problems that might precipitate a runaway. For instance, if concern is developing over the health of a parent at home, it can be diluted by a telephone call from the boy to his mother. Then, this can be explored with the therapist for its meaning. If the staff and the child have a clear understanding of the meaning of one run, the repetition of it as a solution to a new situation can be prevented. It is an important discovery for the child when he finds out that he can learn to exert a degree of self-control, and that he is not completely at the mercy of internal and external forces he does not understand.

SUMMARY

Through the interviews we conducted with the twenty-eight children who had run away from the Spaulding Youth Centre, we discovered that the help of all levels of staff was needed for the children to be able to understand and control their behaviour. We began to give attention to this question at intake and to exclude those who were chronic runaways and those whose running away would be harmful and not therapeutically usable. For those we did accept, we considered the runaway behaviour in planning their programmes. The therapists used their understanding of the children's behaviour both directly, in the therapeutic relationship, and less directly, by serving as consultants to other staff members.

After gaining a degree at the University of Vermont, United States of America, in 1950 Donald S. Farrington received his Master's degree in Social Service from the Boston University School of Social Work in 1958. After a short time as a Field Instructor at this School of Social Work he was for four years Executive Director of the Spaulding Youth Centre in Tilton, New Hampshire, a residential treatment institution for emotionally disturbed children. He is now Executive Director of the United Workers of Norwich, a Family and Children's Service and Public Health Nursing Service in Connecticut.

William R. Shelton M.D. received his medical training at Ohio State University, and spent a year in child training at the Massachusetts General Hospital and the Children's Hospital, becoming a member of the American Board of Psychiatry in 1951. For four years he was chief consultant to the Spaulding Youth Centre and for the past seven years has been chief consultant io the Juvenile Court at Cambridge, Massachusetts.

James R. MacKay studied at Tufts College and Boston University, gaining the degrees of A.M. in Sociology and M.S. in S.S. specializing in psychiatric social work. After spending four years engaged in research for the Massachusetts Youth Service Board, he became in 1958 a social worker at an Alcoholism Clinic in Boston. At the same time he acted as a social work consultant to several residential institutions for delinquents including the Spaulding Youth Centre. In 1960 he was appointed Executive Director of the Programme on Alcoholism and then Co-ordinator of Community Mental Health both in the New Hampshire Department of Health and Welfare. He is currently a psychiatric social worker in private practice and continues to be associated with social work organizations concerned with alcoholism and addiction.

10

Group therapeutic techniques for residential units

Case Conference, vol. 4, no. 7, Janurary 1958.

James Anthony

In this article Professor Anthony engages our interest from the start by contrasting 'beating' with 'treating' as alternative ways of dealing with difficult children. The former method at least gave the child a clear indication of what behaviour was wrong and where the boundaries of misbehaviour lay: the latter demands from the child contrition and restitution. Adults caring for children are however often uncomfortably split in their attitudes, sometimes being provoked to punitive measures when children will not respond to treatment. Professor Anthony described several types of therapeutic groups in residential settings, groups of children and of adolescents, groups of staff and children together, staff groups and parent groups. He shows how in staff groups some conflicting motives may be brought to the surface and helps us to recognize our own need to receive love from children as well as to give it to them.

This paper was adapted from an address given to a study conference of the Association of Workers for Maladjusted Children in 1957.

A little while ago, a cartoon appeared in the *New Yorker* showing a psychiatrist's office. In it sat a mother, looking alert but slightly mystified, and a very sullen, resentful little boy. The psychiatrist was saying to the mother: 'Mrs Minton, there's no such thing as a bad boy. Hostile, perhaps aggressive, recalcitrant, destructive, even sadistic. But not *bad.*'

Now this is the brand of popular confusion that followed on the psycho-analytical discovery of an infantile neurosis. Since Freud, but not because of him, naughtiness for the 'enlightened' parent has yielded place to neurosis; that is to say: a beatable condition has been transformed into a treatable one, a state of sin into a state of being sinned against, and a simple causal relationship between temptation and wrong-doing into a complex, overdetermined and deep disturbance. The child, having been furnished with an unconscious mind, was no longer considered to be a free agent. It was committed to certain inevitable forms of behaviour by the interplay of psychological forces in its early environment. The 'badness' of the child was assumed to be part of the 'badness' of the parent or of the unconscious wish on the part of the parents to be 'bad'; and so the sins of the children were visited on the parents and grandparents in an endless, receding series. It seems, then, that we have almost lost the valuable concept of naughtiness, through which both parent and children learnt to know, the hard way, where they stood with regard to each other. They knew, or felt they knew, each others motives, but with the submergence of motives into the unconscious, behaviour ceased to be explicable in the old reassuring way. Once the child discovered that it was no longer naughty but neurotic, the century of the common child can be said to have dawned. It had become invulnerable.

No psychiatrist has yet been bold enough to work against the current stream of opinion and include naughtiness among the diagnostic categories in use in his clinic, although he might often have felt that it had a justifiable place in the labelling of some cases. The old-fashioned term is sometimes disguised under the euphemism of 'secondary gain', which gives naughtiness a superior status.

These three contemporary attitudes I have mentioned: that the child is not naughty but neurotic; that the environment is to blame and not the child; and that the condition is treatable and not beatable—were obviously designed by the well-meaning to assuage the crippling burden of guilt, but the unfortunate consequences have been that we are dealing with guiltier children than ever before and, what is more, guiltier parents. The emotional consequences of *not* punishing a child when it deserves it, or thinks it deserves it, are often far-reaching ('I always feel I'm getting away with things and I never know how far I can go'). In the old days limits were rigidly set—so far and no further with a very narrow *margin of safety*—but if the parents were *consistent* the child knew the boundaries within which he could 'play up'. Today the middle-class practice of looking aggrieved and withdrawing love has come to

replace the time-honoured and long-respected physical expressions
of anger. The middle-class parents are often paralyzed by guilt and
the children immobilized by fear. A young patient once said to me:
'my mother never raises a hand to any of us; she only has *to look.*'
Well, we all know that sort of look, because, as modern parents,
we practice it every day of our lives. It is a curious mixture of
displeasure, sorrow, resignation, martyrdom and frustration.
When expertly expressed to a really sensitive child, it can have a
devastating effect, and the results can really last, so that the child
may be miserable for days, have difficulty in falling asleep, lose its
appetite temporarily and even have a succession of nightmares.
The old-fashioned beating, given in the heat of the moment could
seldom claim to achieve as much. The psychological technique, in
contrast to the physical one, demands, from the child an appropriate
quantum of guilt, contrition, promises of amendment and possibly
compulsive and ritualistic practices of restitution. When the
negative parental feeling is immeasurable or inconsistent (because
they do strike out when goaded beyond bearing) there is no amount
of restitution that can give the child a feeling of security. The
'ironing out' of the cues of emotional expression by the inhibited
parent can give rise to an extremely fearful child unable to gauge
the strength of feeling either in himself or in others.

I have been discussing this curious twentieth-century attitude in
terms of parents, but the same applies to parent-substitutes, 'house
parents', teachers, nurses, case-workers, therapists or to any form
of surrogation. Most of us, except the very youngest, have had a
punitive upbringing by today's standard. We have all been beaten
in the past, and, under previous conditions, could have reasonably
expected to do some beating ourselves in the future. But this was
not to be. A new ethos had invaded the world. We were now
expected not to beat but to treat. Nevertheless, the beating was
there inside all of us, and we had to come to terms with the past in
order to deal with the present; that is, most of us needed to be
treated before we could treat, and so some of us (the analysts)
undertook to be treated in order that we could treat. Our children,
therefore, were to remain unbeaten however strongly they wished
to be beaten and had phantasies about being beaten. We were to
suppress the complementary tendency in ourselves and manage
the children 'psychologically'. The untreated have often absorbed

this new ethos without working through it, and the result has been that they have remained uncomfortably split; the latent, unconscious desires were to beat but the adult, sophisticated view point condemned this impulse as sadistic and struggled with itself to spare the rod and save the child. The latent, punitive tendency may seep out indirectly whenever the child becomes unresponsive or negativistic. We then resort to physical measures 'for its own good' although it hurts us so much more. The child very soon comes to know who wants to beat it and does not, who wants to treat it and cannot, and who imagines that he is treating it by beating it. The beaten child is learning slowly inside himself to become a beater.

An adolescent boy, badly beaten in childhood, told me that he was determined to have lots of children himself in order to be able to beat them. I asked whether this would not make them unhappy. He agreed that it would but *only* whilst they were children. Once they were grown-up they could beat their own children and become happy again.

The attitude of the *lex talionis* is very easily inculcated in childhood by such mechanisms of revenge and identification with the aggressor.

It is not so easy to distinguish sharply between naughtiness and neurosis because the two are often intermingled. Naughty children can be neurotic, and neurotic children naughty. If it is not so easy to separate the naughty from the neurotic, it is even less easy to separate the need for beating from the need for treating. It would be logical to beat the naughty and treat the neurotic if we could make sure who were naughty and who neurotic and for what inner or outer reasons we were beating them or treating them. For many parents it is also important to decide whether to beat in 'cold blood' or 'hot blood', because for them spontaneity makes the attack on the child more forgivable.

The whole question is a highly complex one and particularly difficult for the adult and child to cope with under the usual conditions. To my mind the great advantage of the group situation is that this relationship between the beater and beaten and treater and treated can be brought to a therapeutic focus and the latent guilt on both sides fully exposed.

For some years now, I have been using group methods with

in-patient units and with the mothers of the children. I have used them for all sorts of purposes in addition to treatment, although treatment has always been the major purpose. Whenever I wanted to find out how things were going in the ward, what the children felt about the staff, what the staff felt about the children, where the disturbances that periodically upset the unit originated, and so on, I sampled the situation with a group. If I wanted to know more about a particular symptom, I took a group of children manifesting such symptoms or mothers of such children; I found it was the quickest way to learn about it.

Now why does one learn so much from a group and so quickly? I think it is mainly because the usual one-to-one clinic situation forces the child to defend himself against the intensive, and concentrated, and focussed explorations of the therapist. In the group the child has support from the others and attention for the therapist diluted and in addition he has to face the eternal problem of childhood–the sibling situation. By watching the children together I not only learn how child A reacts or how child B reacts but, what is often much more important, how child A *interacts* with child B, and the third person, the therapist is then in a position to observe this interaction, objectively, because he is not directly involved in it. In the one-to-one situation you have to be well trained and well treated before you can observe with any degree of objectivity and detachment. In the group it is easier to achieve this, especially if one's therapeutic aims are modest.

For groups, as with all therapeutic procedures, one requires a certain amount of time and a certain amount of space; one requires regularity, because it is then easier to detect irregularity, and one requires a certain number of people, but not too many or too few. One should aim, generally, at not less than five and not more than ten. Next, one wants it not too widely spaced with respect to age; I usually aim at having not more than two years between the children. I also like some equality with respect to intelligence; the forward and backward don't mix very well or very helpfully. On the whole I try to avoid having any child with a unique tendency or condition, as he is so easily transformed into a scapegoat. I like, however, a nice balance of temperaments and personalities–of active and passive, of outgoing and inhibited, of manic and depressive, of hysterical and obsessional. Lastly I make sure that the child fully and clearly understands what he is in the group for, and what I am up to. This is not play and not school. I say to him 'This is *your* treatment.' I make it as clear to the group as I would to a child I was treating psycho-analytically.

A short while ago, I was taking a session, on a case of enuresis that had been coming up for months. The doctor, who presented the case to me, had been treating the child for some time by means of drawing and painting. The patient had not been doing too well, as testified by the wet nights, and, in response to maternal pressure the doctor had fallen for the somatic defence; he put the child on benzedrine tablets. I asked the boy what he felt about his treatment and he said: 'It's all right; it's not too difficult to swallow!' I then asked him if he did anything else when he came up, and he replied: 'Oh yes, they let me paint to pass the time whilst I'm waiting for my tablets.' In the children's groups I try and make sure at least that they know what they are supposed to swallow!

The way in which the groups are run depends very much on the ages concerned; the pre-school groups are given an interest in a play situation. I have invented a special circular sand table for the purposes, divided into five places. Each child has thus its own territory which it can defend or expand, and toy equipment that allows him both to stay behind his own walls or co-operate with his neighbours by means of ladders and tunnels etc. Group formations occur at the level of collective phantasy.[1] In the latency groups, on the other hand, groupings take place at the level of collective activity. As the younger ones expressed conflicts in symbols, so the middle-sized ones express them in action, and in place of symbolic interpretation, we use action interpretation. In the adolescent groups, the children, for the first time, can be coaxed into sitting around in a circle and expressing things verbally, and so interpretations are of the verbal themes brought up by members. Now, I mention interpretations because they are one of the main dynamic trimmings to the group therapeutic process; it is one side, the analytic side of the treatment. But the supportive and interactive aspects are as important and these require no special training or expertise; a 'therapeutic personality' plus a bit of experience will usually suffice. Understanding and experience

[1] E. J. Anthony and S. H. Foulkes, *Group Psychotherapy from the Psychoanalytic point of view*, Penguin Books, 1957.

with children can take one a long way in the use of group techniques.

I come next to the second type of sub-group that one can envisage in a residential unit—the staff-children group, composed of equal numbers of staff and children expressing their opinions frankly to each other. These groups are not difficult for the staff to handle because they feel bolstered up by their colleagues, but, however evenly the numbers are distributed, the children will inevitably, at the beginning, feel out-numbered and at a disadvantage. In this type of group the grievances of the children and the counter-grievances of the staff are made the centre of the discussion. Complaints are positive contributions, if they are treated in reciprocal fashion—a two-way process with bilateral systems of respect and understanding at work. The children need to understand the difficulties of the staff and *vice versa*.

In one such group in which I was a staff-representative member, a little girl said: 'Don't you sometimes feel that you would like to give us all a good bashing. If I were you I would want to or else I'd explode. It must be awful to keep it all inside you!' Now the immediate response to the girl's remarks was a series of defences put forward by the staff members against the suggestion that staff could have negative feelings *at all*. They were there, they said, for the good of the children. Because of their completely adult status and maturity, and because of their enormous professional permissiveness and tolerance, their only reactions lay in the direction of greater understanding of the child, 'We are here to understand you,' said one, 'that's our job: if we were to become cross we would fail in our jobs.' The jobs, it seemed gave them this superhuman ability not to feel the daily pricks and arrows of outrageous children. There was no room for counter-transference. Now the child assumed that the staff felt the same as she did but concealed it better. She seemed to be saying 'If I were you, I would feel cross, so where has the crossness gone?' And that's the question: Where *had* the crossness gone? I agreed with the children that it must have gone *somewhere*; had the staff become more tense, more anxious, more persecuted, more negativistic, more pompous; had they kicked the institution's cat, or developed migraine, abdominal pain or pains in the neck?

Such defence mechanisms against sexual and aggressive feelings towards the children can be obliquely dealt with in the staff groups. These groups need specially to be run by an outsider with no emotional axe to grind for himself and with a reasonable degree of non-involvement in the maelstrom of residential life.

One could approach the matter initially by discussing certain assumptions:

1. That all of us who take up this sort of work generally have deep unconscious reasons for it. Our motives may be directed by our own disturbances, by our unsatisfied needs and by desires to make restitution for some deep misdoing. Sometimes these disturbances could affect our relationship with the children–resonating, as it were, in sympathy with theirs.

2. That there is nothing intrinsically wrong with feeling feelings, even socially-unacceptable feelings. But we all tend to defend ourselves against such feelings. Some of us may do it in hysterical ways, by identifying too closely with our charges; others might become over-anxious without admitting to any definite focus of anxiety–just a 'free-floating anxiety'; others may make use of obsessional and rigid attitudes, that often disguise sadistic and sexual wishes; others might deny their difficulties completely or else project them on to children or on to other members of the staff so that a scapegoat becomes necessary. These are universal mechanisms, so who is going to cast the first stone? Well, every member of the staff group will want to do so, since the best means of defence in psychological as in physical warfare is attack. With staff, I have found that even a superficial analysis of these defending and attacking mechanisms–the mechanisms of attack are as many and as varied and as disguised as the mechanisms of defence –can lead to an opening up of current conflicts. In any groups, there is usually a mixed assortment of attackers and defenders, the attackers attacking, and not aware that they are attacking or trying to conceal this intention or even denying it; the defenders defending, and not knowing that they were defending and denying that they have anything to be defensive about. Confronting the group with its naked intentions is one of the factors that could lead to the disruption of the group, but the truth in therapy need never be made too suddenly or too shockingly. In these quasi-therapeutic situations, I like to counsel the well-known political

course of *gradualism*. All these matters can be learned deeply and meaningfully and slowly. Since Freud, no one has ever been in a hurry with psycho-therapy. The best treatment is 'interminable' (Freud's expression) or else it feels like it!

3. The third assumption is that there is a need to give and take in all human relationships. Sometimes we give too much and feel resentful, or take too much and feel greedy but, in general, most of us enjoy both rôles. Whenever we come to deal with patients or children, some of us begin to think that we have only to give and no longer take. It is true that maladjusted children can be exceedingly demanding, and drain us of our feeling with parasitic pleasure, giving little or nothing back in return, but no unilateral relationship in human society is a good one. It may be better to give than to receive, but unilateral giving is bad for both sides. It is always therapeutically wise to expect something in return, even from the most psychotic child, for whom the act of giving may become the act of redemption. Any human being, who allows himself to be constantly treated as a cupboard, will eventually find it as bare as that of Mother Hubbard. He has a duty to himself to replenish his stores of love from time to time.

Many caretakers of children believe it to be their official purpose to drain themselves of feeling for the sake of the children, like some self-sacrificing mothers. They see themselves as givers, asking nothing in return, and this is what they consider so admirably therapeutic—that their loving is unconditional. Such an attitude, on analysis, frequently reveals itself as a defence against an inner feelings of greed. They have to do something for nothing because they want everything. In the group, no attempt is made to analyse such primitive reactions, but their existence can be profitably pointed out. It should be shown.

(*a*) That unilateral receiving is not therapeutic for the child.
(*b*) That unilateral giving is not healthy for the adult.
(*c*) That the establishment of a reciprocal relationship is as good an end point to short-term therapy as any.
(*d*) That the period of service of unilateral givers is shorter than it should be.

The structuring of an institution through groups may serve a number of important functions.

In the first place, it gives everyone an experience of the same therapeutic environment (and all doctors benefit from a taste of their own medicine). It cuts across such false dichotomies as You and Me, staff and patient, adult and child, treater and treated, giver and receiver. When discussing growing up, Ruth Benedict introduced the important concept of continuity and discontinuity of development; if development was too discontinuous; if there was too big a gap between one phase of development and another, the desire to mature might fail e.g. too wide a gap between the sexless child and the sexuality of the adult, or between the submission of the child and the authority of the adult, then the child might be unable to pass from one state to the other.

The same concept could well apply to the hierarchies of an institution; the gap between staff and child should not be too wide. Where the staff is composed of maids and cooks and cleaners and teachers and therapists and so forth and all are integrated under the term staff, then the adult-child discontinuity and the authoritarian outlook stemming from it may be considerably reduced. The type of adult that serves one's meals, or washes one's pants or gossips to one in the kitchen is not so distant generally as the type of adult who teaches one geometry, disciplines one, or sounds one's chest with a stethescope. A range of such adults may give the child this important sense of continuity and this can be aided and abetted by the use of groups.

The next valuable use of a group organization is in the early localization of disturbances, so that they no longer occur suddenly, unexpectedly and catastrophically. The latent life of a community can be rendered more manifest, and the collective unconscious give place to a collective consciousness. The institution organized on group lines has, as it were, a number of radar mechanisms operating so that a minimal disturbance can be easily picked up. The same staff member will be participating in the children's groups, in the staff-children groups, and in the staff groups. If any section of the community is disturbed by interpersonal difficulties, it will soon be abundantly clear at what level the disturbance is acting, what the content of that disturbance is, what the pattern of the disturbance is and how large and intense it is.

By pattern I mean the dynamic interpersonal configuration, the number of interlocking personnel. What has been called a *configurational analysis* involves determining the nature and extent of the interaction and the localization of the centre of the disturbance.

In an institutional setting one of the male staff smacked a child. There was an administrative outcry, and the man was immediately shifted from the unit. In a mixed group of children, the incident occupied a whole session. The children were indignant about the matter. They wanted me to take sides and express an opinion. Did I agree with children being smacked? I said I personally did not smack children, but many parents did and felt they were doing the right thing. I asked them what they felt about this, and, to a child, they were against it. Children should never be smacked because it hurt them. I pointed out that this was what the parents intended; but then, one of the children remarked that it was often worse to be scolded. 'That,' said another child, 'is only because there is something the matter with our minds: it makes us sensitive.' What she objected to was that the smack had been on the bottom; that was very undignified. 'They think you can treat a child anyway you like. Mr P only beat John, because he was teasing him about kissing Mrs X.' This was the first hint that the children knew something more than they had previously let out. When asked about the kissing, they had supported John because they did not like Mr P.

In the staff group that followed, the members were also highly indignant about the situation, especially because Mr P had been removed. The boy had been asking for it for a long time, they said; he was a real trouble-maker; he was not maladjusted; he was just a malingerer. They also tried to induce me to take sides: did I think it was fair that a member of the staff should be removed unheard just because he struck a bad boy for using a very dirty word with regard to Mrs X. When I asked what the word was, Mrs X blushed and said she would rather the matter was forgotten. (The word, I discovered later, was prostitute.)

In a mothers' group shortly after, the mother of the boy said to me: 'I hear he got hit by one of the staff; I can quite understand why; he is really a most provocative boy. Just before he was admitted, I gave him a smack and he said that he would tell his father that he had caught me kissing the milkman. I had to give him half-a-crown even though it was quite untrue. I knew what a

suspicious man my husband was!' So far it appeared therefore:

1. That the child used the same threat with the nurse when he got
   smacked, as he did with his mother when he got half-a-crown.
2. That without seeing any smoke, he had diagnosed a fire and
   then fabricated the smoke. Was this also true in the case of his
   mother?
3. The children had known it to be untrue but wanted to get an
   unpopular member of the staff into trouble.

In a final mixed group of staff and children some time after, the
boy admitted to the staff members that he had made up the story and
when they asked him why he had done it, he replied: 'It's what I
always imagined they were doing. When I first came in here I
imagined all the men and women were having sex together and
couldn't get it out of my mind. I thought Mrs X shouldn't do that
sort of thing because she had children.' This is as good an example
of transference in childhood as one could find.

The example illustrates among other things how useful a
mothers' group can be to complement the groups of the unit, the
complex relationship between outside and inside worlds, past and
present, adult and child, parent and parent-surrogate is made
fairly clear. It illustrates the operation of a group technique, the
ramifications of a disturbance through a community and its
localization in the outside world of one of the children. Finally it
reveals the unconscious knowledge that people in residential
establishments accumulate about each other.

SUMMARY

Within the last ten years, a new psychotherapeutic technique,
midway between individual and community therapy, has been
successfully practised under clinic and hospital conditions. Its
further application to residential units, not geared to a staff of
qualified therapists, raises many questions of theoretical and
practical interest.

The technique is directed towards the resolution of interpersonal problems confronting small groups whose composition can

be maintained over a certain minimal period of time. The treatment effects may be multiplied by increasing the number of groups to a point at which every individual in the community has been assimilated into one or more of them, and the activities of these small groups can then be co-ordinated with the wider community programme.

Every sub-group of a residential unit is, to varying degrees, amenable to this line of therapy, but the different systems of relationship (child-child; staff-child; staff-parent; staff-staff; staff-visiting psychiatrists, social workers or psychologists) would offer different types of difficulty in making groups, maintaining them, and using them to the best therapeutic advantage.

The various groups would be, for the most part, self-governing, although always needing some unobstructive form of 'conducting' or chairmanship. They would be regarded as voluntary associations that had come together willingly for a common therapeutic purpose, and would be kept together by the development of an autonomous group life. The groups would cut across the established hierarchies of a residential community.

The 'key group', and the one most difficult to run, would undoubtedly be the staff group, which might do a lot better with an outside conductor, say a visiting psychiatrist or P.S.W. This would make for the most economic and effective use of such a person, when he was available.

Because of the 'common denominators' there would be a great deal of mutual influence at work between the groups so that the latent psychological life of the community would gradually become more manifest and disturbance more easily localized.

'Levels' of treatment would assume that all sections could do with some of it, but that the intensity would vary with the nature of the group. The children's group would enjoy a full therapeutic experience with the possibility of abreacting both positive and negative feelings. The child's point of view would be presented to other children. In the staff-child groups, the conditions would again be reciprocal, so that the child's point of view would be fully presented to the staff and *vice versa*. The staff group would understandably have a limited therapeutic purpose and the word 'treatment' may perhaps be wisely eschewed from its context. Their meetings would focus on special difficulties with children and on difficulties with special children, and the aim, as with other groups, would not be primarily to create insight or explore a deeper motivation, but to undergo in common with others, a 'corrective emotional experience'.

Five questions remain to be answered:

1. Would the inadequacies of staffing ultimately defeat any such therapeutic programme, even were it possible to begin it?
2. Could untrained personnel participate rewardingly in such a programme.
3. Are staff groups run on quasi-therapeutic lines feasible in a residential establishment.
4. Should they be conducted by an 'outsider' rather than a staff member?
5. Are there dangers to such therapeutic programmes, such as would cause the staff justifiably to complain or leave.

These can only be answered in the light of further experience.

E. James Anthony received his medical, psychiatric and psychoanalytic education in London. In 1950 to 1952 he worked with Jean Piaget in Switzerland on child development, and from 1952 to 1958 he was Senior Lecturer in child psychiatry at the University of London and Consultant Psychiatrist to the Maudsley Hospital. He also lectured on family psychology to social work students (including child care officers) at the London School of Economics. He has specialized in group work with children, adolescents, parents and families and is co-author with Dr S. H. Foulkes of 'Group Psychotherapy from the psycho-analytic point of view' (Penguin Books, 1957). He is currently Professor of Child Psychiatry at the Washington University School of Medicine, St Louis, Missouri, United States of America.

I I
Psychiatric consultation in residential treatment: the child care worker's view

The American Journal of Orthopsychiatry, vol. 28, no. 2, April 1958.

Mary Jean Riley

In the previous article Professor Anthony discusses some of the therapeutic benefits of staff groups and in his final paragraphs raises a few questions relating to difficulties that arise. He suggests that more experience is needed before these questions can be answered. Some of this experience is provided in the article which now follows. Miss Riley describes how a group consultation session enabled her to gain a deeper understanding of a seriously disturbed girl called Jane. She further obtained a clearer awareness of some of her own personal attributes, which enabled her to provide Jane with a relationship which could help her on the road to more positive mental health.

When a group of us, who are counsellors at the Orthogenic School, congregate for our midnight snack and coffee, we nearly always chat about the children whom we have just put safely to sleep; about the funny, unusual, or exasperating things that happened during the day. We talk to each other to unwind, to understand better what occurred during the day, and to bring each other up-to-date on what is going on in the rest of the institution. As we relax, we also gradually become more serious about our problems; our talk is more intimate as we search within ourselves, with each other's help, for likely reasons for the difficulties we encountered during the day, and for the possible solutions to them. This may bring to mind one or more of the staff meetings which we had recently or sometimes months ago with our consultants. I think that for every worker, teacher, counsellor, nurse, or what not, there are certain meetings that, for a long time, remain vividly in the mind.

As we work at the Orthogenic School over the years, our conception of the School and ourselves is constantly changing, along with our feelings and ideas about staff meetings. The meeting which will serve as illustration of a continuous and complex process is one that occurred many months ago, but which still has consequences for me and for the child we discussed, as well as for other workers who are concerned either with this girl or with children presenting similar problems.

This meeting took place shortly after a major change in dormitory groupings. In one of our groups, the girls who had been living together for some years had developed so unevenly that our programming and activities no longer seemed appropriate to them all. After much thought and hesitation–a change in dormitory placement is, in our setting, among the most serious decisions we have to make–we had concluded that it would be best for the entire group if the three older girls were moved into another dormitory to form the nucleus of a new group. Jane, who was one of the younger girls, was not be be moved. My co-counsellor, to whom Jane was much attached (though not necessarily more so than to me), went along with the three older girls to take care of them in the new group. I, who had been Jane's counsellor for many years–in fact from the day she came–remained with her in the old group, of whom Jane was the eldest.

One of the reasons why we felt that Jane should remain in the younger group was that we wanted to counteract her tendency to pseudo-maturity. However, following this change in grouping, she began to assume a rather maternal rôle with the younger children, an attitude about which I was becoming increasingly uncomfortable. At the same time, this seemed not to be the sole or complete cause of my discomfort.

In this particular staff meeting, the consultant recalled that when he had previously seen Jane on one of his regular visits to the dormitory, she had acted adequate and even somewhat like a counsellor, but that there had been what he felt was an underlying sulkiness and childish petulance about her which he expected to emerge at any moment. This morning, however, Jane seemed depressed and apathetic with him. The way she kept her distance from him, as well as her stuttering, suggested to the consultant that she was frightened of being observed by him. However, she finally mentioned the younger children spontaneously when she told him that, on the previous night, she had asked one of them to undress her. Jane felt very guilty about this. Though she did not refer specifically to the sexual pleasure which she seemed to have gotten from it, this was present as an undertone. Jane also said that she had been angry with another child who was closer to her own age, but had felt unable to express this anger, and then had 'taken it out' on the younger girl.

Jane also mentioned her coming fourteenth birthday. She spoke of having volunteered recently, on a Sunday, to help the cooks with their work in the kitchen, and described how she had lifted trays for one of them who wasn't feeling well. This reminded the consultant of the fact that Jane's mother had suffered for years from multiple sclerosis, so that helping an older woman repeated many of Jane's past experiences. He mentioned that asking another child to undress her the previous night might have some relation to her mother's need to have others dress and undress her.

I then spoke about how concerned I felt when Jane helped with the younger children. On the one hand, it seemed to give her some real satisfaction and vicarious pleasure, since she cared for them as she would like to be cared for. But on the other hand, it had led to events such as those described. I had similar doubts about her working in the kitchen.

Jane's former counsellor, who continued to see her twice a week in play sessions, added that, in asking another child to undress her, it seemed as though Jane were making an invalid of herself, like her mother. But to Jane, being an invalid also meant to be helpless, and to be cared for like a baby. Jane had told us that she suspected she was kept in the younger group as a punishment for her wish to be a baby. Her notion all along had been that to be a baby is bad.

Our conversation led Jane's teacher to speak about the notice-able slump in Jane's work in the class since the change in grouping. She had seemed quite despondent in class, and was spending much of her time daydreaming.

At this point the director stressed that, in speaking of her mother's illness, Jane always called it 'capital' rather than multiple sclerosis, although she had often been told the correct term. The director thought that, through the dissipation of energy in various 'helpful' activities (only some of which she had described to the consultant), Jane kept herself busy acting out the 'good little girl'; while at other times she acted out the helpless infant, the indolent 'dummy' who did not know what was going on, the petulant child, and so on. In this way she kept herself, as it were, in a state of 'multiple psychosis' instead of permitting herself to have a 'capital' one. Since the mother suffered from a 'capital illness'–that is, terminal, as Jane knew–Jane, by never connecting herself to anything central, anything 'capital', seemed to be defending herself against her fear of becoming incapacitated and deathly sick, like her mother. She was safe as long as she lived a vague, disorganized, 'multiple' life. On the other hand, she could never get hold of, and master, something so diffuse as her multiple self. For this and many other reasons, she had been embarking on various defensive manoeuvres. We had made the mistake of fostering some of them, instead of encouraging her to experience her truly 'capital' feelings of deep, underlying depression.

The director felt that the crucial event in Jane's life at this time was the fact that, at long last, she had not been moved. The pattern of her life, practically from birth on, had been that of a long series of foster homes and school placements. This time, however, she had remained stationary while other children had been moved. But at the same time, she had been deserted by one of her main counsellors.

I interrupted to say that I did not need to be reminded that Jane was depressive–a remark which hinted at my own depressive tendencies and reflected my vivid recollections of the prolonged depression out of which Jane had emerged in the not-too-distant past. My underlying feelings were that she had only very recently begun to come out of her depression and that she should be encouraged and helped to do so successfully.

In answer to my statement, the director described Jane's manoeuvres–such as her teasing of her former counsellor, her working in the kitchen, or her helping with the other children–as attempts to prove to herself that she was alive, that she was not dying of the terrible disease from which her mother suffered, or from some other terminal illness. But in being so defensively active, Jane was dissipating her very limited emotional capital. To do many things meant to her to be alive; but what she really wanted most of all was not to have to move. He concluded that, to him, Jane's life history seemed one big fight against what some psychoanalysts called the 'depressive position'.

This reminded me of the way Jane was when she had first come to us: unwilling to make any move, fighting any suggestion that she leave the dormitory, terribly frightened of any kind of activity, having to carry food around with her whenever she moved away from her bed. Gradually, over the years, she had become more comfortable, but now I realized that she had probably learned to look more comfortable than she felt in many of her activities. Certainly her experiments in trying to lead a more normally active life left her totally exhausted; that was why she always threw herself on her bed at the conclusion of any of her short-lived spurts of activity. For the first time I fully realized what a relief it must be for Jane to be living in a group where she could be more inactive, where life proceeded on a more infantile level. But this projected her even more deeply into an impasse, in that when she experienced the relief which came with doing nothing, she also became terrified, because not to move was to her not to be alive, to be dying as her mother was dying.

As the conversation went on, and as each of the staff members working with Jane presented supporting evidence, we gradually realized that the most constructive measure for Jane would be to make her feel so secure that her close relation to us in itself would permit her to feel alive, though otherwise she did not move at all. Then, we felt, she could afford to experience herself, which was a self in extreme depression, rather than frantically having to defend herself against this experience. We decided that Jane could permit herself to feel and live her depression if she were convinced that we could protect her against being totally swallowed up by it. If this could be called a recommendation, the result of the staff meeting was that Jane should be made so secure that she could be openly depressed.

This still left unresolved the big question of whether we would be able to make this possible for Jane. The circumstances which the dormitory move had brought about were favourable to such an enterprise. The unanswered question was whether those of us who worked with Jane were ready to accept her depression, to stay with her in it, and eventually to bring her out of it. The question thus became: How frightened were we of becoming intimately familiar with living in a depression, hers and our own?

This staff meeting ended just before lunch. When the staff feels that matters have remained unresolved, that answerable questions have remained unanswered, then the issues evoked during the meeting are discussed through lunch and into the afternoon. After this meeting, however, there seemed little to say about the essential points, which were clear to those of us who were most concerned. Each person had to decide individually what he would be able to do, and the answer to the problem could only lie in the way we would carry out our decisions.

Up to the time of this meeting, I had been worried about whether Jane's needs would be adequately met in the dormitory grouping we had provided for her. I was quite unsure about the wisdom of keeping her in my group of younger children. The outcome of the meeting for me was that it now seemed a real possibility that retaining her in my dormitory could be of great, positive value to her; and also (what I had not realized before) that, in addition to my long and warm interest in Jane, I had certain personal attributes or inclinations that could be of help to her.

Before going on duty with my group that afternoon, I changed my clothes. As I met Jane's former counsellor in the hall, she commented that I had changed to a predominantly black outfit; I had not been aware of this. We both laughed, with some anxiety, and I said, 'Well now I am preparing for the depression.'

The group was to go swimming that day, an activity that had been highly important to Jane until a few months ago, when she had passed the deep water test. Since then, she had lost all interest in swimming and had refused to go with us.

I had anticipated that she would refuse on this day, too, but now I had a different attitude about it. I didn't want to force her into any more activities. So when she again said that she didn't want to go swimming, and asked if I would make her, I told her, 'I would like you to be with me, but I want even more that you do what you want to do.' Jane was thrown off balance by this, and tried to press me into making some decision for her. I only repeated what I had said, and waited. After several minutes of indecision and actually moving back and forth from me to her bed, she decided to come. As we walked to the pool, she was quite enthusiastic about going and held my hand most of the way.

However, at the pool she again said that she would not go in the water, but would put on her bathing suit. After I had been in the water, for a while, playing with some of the younger children, I called to Jane and asked if she wanted to come in, too. She complained that it was too cold; however, if I would lift her into the pool, as I did the little children, she would come in, but only if I would also keep her mostly out of the water. I did this, and she stayed in the pool with me for the rest of the period, holding on to my back with her arms around my neck and remaining unusually quiet. In fact, her whole body was extremely limp, as though she were exhausted and wanted to rest against me.

I was surprised and really didn't understand what had happened with Jane during that day. I couldn't see the connection between what she had done and the conclusions of the meeting, because I had expected that she would retire into isolated passivity. So naturally I discussed what happened after I came off duty. Thus our morning staff conversation continued that night. The director pointed out to me that what had happened was pretty much what had been discussed in the meeting. Jane having been given permission to be depressed, had gone back to the most babyish of situations, being cradled in my arms in the water, being completely dependent on me; and this feeling had continued throughout the rest of the day, when she was much closer to me than she had been for many weeks.

Either because of my clearer understanding, or for some other reason, Jane was now able to do things more *her* way. A few days later she took advantage of a visit to the dentist to take to her bed for the greater part of the day. During this time she enjoyed having me prepare food for her, feed her, and fuss over her as though she were really sick. Another day, she claimed that she had a stomachache, took to bed again, and equally enjoyed being babied.

Since then Jane has continued to feel more strongly both her depression and her enjoyment of infantile pleasures. Progress is still very slow, often being held up by her fear, and our own, of going too deeply into depressive passivity, so that even now, at this writing, about half a year later, we have not concluded our common voyage through the nether world, nor have we yet come back entirely to the 'world of the living'.

But this staff meeting, in which we arrived at what was right for Jane, still comes to my mind each day that I am with her, and continues to be the focus of what I try to do for and with her.

When we talked about what the meetings with out consultants mean to the workers of the School, this particular staff meeting came to mind almost simultaneously to Jane's former counsellor and to me. It continues to underlie many of our conversations about Jane and our attempts to understand our work with her. In preparing these remarks, about six months after this meeting, we found that we fully recalled only a few important sentences that had been said. But we retained the stong emotional impression the meeting had created in us. These feelings about Jane became more and more meaningful as we realized that they were enabling us to participate better in her emotional development during the months following the meeting, and to become much more sensitive to her vital needs.

Encountering a child and ourselves in this way leads to a re-evaluation, sometimes to a change, and occasionally to fireworks. The outcome of such a meeting can be painful or unpleasant. It is always unpredictable and potentially far-reaching. Since this particular meeting, in which we saw Jane's dilemma so clearly and realized how we could help her better, she has become even more important to us in a more personal way. I, for one, in my work with her have been more myself, and as a result Jane has become more herself. We all feel that this is a pretty good outcome for one staff meeting.

After graduating at Notre Dame Academy, Toledo, Ohio and receiving the degree of A.B. from Mary Manse College, Toledo, Mary Jean Riley, now Mary Jean Riley Key, taught for two years in elementary schools in U.S.A. She then joined the staff of the Sonia Shankman Orthogenic School of the University of Chicago, known to many English readers through the books of Dr Bruno Bettelheim, and served as a Counsellor-Research Assistant until February 1961, a period of more than ten years. She is married to Glenn Shelton Key, a social worker, and is the mother of two boys and has recently completed an additional year's study at the Chicago Institute for Early Childhood Education.

Further Reading

AICHHORN, AUGUST *Wayward youth*, Hogarth Press, 1957, paperback, Viking Press, 1965.

ALT, HERSCHEL *Residential treatment for the disturbed child*, International Universities Press, New York, 1960.

BALBERNIE, RICHARD *Residential work with children*, Pergamon Press, 1966.

BETTELHEIM, BRUNO *Love is not enough; the treatment of emotionally disturbed children*, Free Press, Glencoe, and Allen & Unwin, 1959; paperback, Collier Books, New York, 1965.

—— *Truants from life: rehabilitation of emotionally disturbed children*, Collier-Macmillan, 1955, paperback, Free Press, 1964.

BURN, MICHAEL *Mr Lyward's answer*, Hamish Hamilton, 1956; paperback, 1964.

DOCKAR–DRYSDALE, B. E. *Papers on residential work: Therapy in child care*, Longmans, 1968.

—— *Consultation in Child Care*, Longman, 1973.

HOME OFFICE ADVISORY COUNCIL ON CHILD CARE *Care and Treatment in a Planned Environment*, H.M.S.O., 1970.

JONES, HOWARD *Reluctant rebels*, Tavistock Publications, 1962.

KING, ROY D., RAYNES, NORMA V. and TIZARD, JACK *Patterns of Residential Care: Sociological studies in institutions for handicapped children*, Routledge and Kegan Paul, 1971.

KONOPKA, GISELA *Group work in the institution*, Whiteside & Morrow, New York, 1954.

—— *Therapeutic group work with children*, University of Minnesota Press, 1949.

LENNHOFF, F. G. *Exceptional children*, Allen & Unwin, 1960.

MCCORKLE, LLOYD W., ELIAS, ALBERT and BIXBY, F. LOVELL *The Highfields Story*, Henry Holt, New York, 1958.

MILLER, DEREK *Growth to freedom*, Tavistock Publications, 1964.

—— 'A model of an institution for treating adolescent delinquent boys' pp. 97–115 in *Changing concepts of crime and its treatment*, Pergamon Press, 1966.

REDL, FRITZ *When we deal with children, Selected writings*, The Free Press, New York; Collier-Macmillan, London, 1966.

Further reading

REDL, FRITZ, and WINEMAN, DAVID *Children who hate: the disorganization and breakdown of behaviour controls*, Free Press, Glencoe, and Allen & Unwin, 1951; paperback, Free Press, 1962.
—— *Controls from within*, Free Press, Glencoe, 1952; paperback, Collier-Macmillan, 1965.
ROSE, GORDON *Schools for young offenders*, Tavistock Publications, 1967.
POLSKY, HOWARD, *Cottage Six*, Wiley, 1962.
POLSKY, H. W. and GLASTER, D. S. *The Dynamics of Residential Treatment*, University of North Carolina Press, 1958.
SHAW, OTTO L. *Maladjusted boys*, Allen & Unwin, 1965.
SHIELDS, ROBERT W. *A cure for delinquents*, Heinemann, 1962.
SLAVSON, S. R. *Re-educating the delinquent through group and community participation*, Collier Books, New York, 1961.
STREET, DAVID, VINTER, ROBERT D. and FERROW, CHARLES *Organisation for Treatment*, Free Press, New York; Collier-Macmillan, London, 1966.
WILLS, DAVID *Throw away the rod*, Gollancz, 1960.
— *A place like home; a hostel for disturbed adolescents*, Allen & Unwin, 1970.
— *Spare the child: the story of an experimental approved school*, Penguin, 1971.
WINNICOT, D. W. 'Group Influences and the Maladjusted Child' Chapter 17 in *The family and individual development*, Tavistock Publications, 1965.

Glossary of technical terms

ABREACT *v.* to release repressed emotions by reliving them in feeling and expressing them

AFFECT *n.* feeling tone accompanying an idea or experience; feeling, emotion or mood

AMBIVALENCE *n.* contradictory feelings felt at the same time e.g. loving and hating

ANOMIE *n.* the state of mind of one who lacks both a sense of obligation to others and an awareness of personal continuity; hence ANOMIC, *adj.*

AUTISM *n.* pathological condition occurring in children who from early childhood are extremely withdrawn, self-absorbed and unable to form relationships; hence AUTISTIC, *adj.*

COLLATERAL *adj.* concurrent.

CONFIGURATION *n.* an organized whole influenced by the inter-relationships of its members, but more than the sum of its parts

CONSTRUCTS *n.* hypothetical categories

COUNSELLOR *n.* residential worker in American treatment homes or institutions

DEPERSONALIZATION *n.* 1. (page 5) a situation where e.g. rules are based on routine procedures rather than personal demands
n. 2. (page 23) the condition of a patient who loses his feeling of the reality of himself as a person

HOMEOSTASIS tendency to maintain an emotional balance or to return to it after disturbance; hence HOMEOSTATIC, *adj.*

HYPOMANIC *adj.* restless, over-active, excitable

INTERPRETATION *n.* the expression, usually in words, by a psychotherapist of a patient's feelings or fantasies of which the patient was previously not fully aware

LIBIDO *n.* force or energy deriving from the love instinct and directed towards a person who becomes the object of a love relationship; hence LIBIDINAL, *adj.*

OBJECT RELATIONSHIP relationship with person with whom one has close emotional ties and who becomes the object or source of satisfaction of unconscious libidinal needs

OEDIPUS COMPLEX unconscious feeling of attachment (basically sexual in character) of boy towards his mother or of girl towards her father accompanied by jealousy of other parent and consequent feelings of guilt; hence OEDIPAL, *adj.*

PARANOIA *n.* delusion of being persecuted

REPETITION COMPULSION impulse to re-enact earlier experiences and situations

SECONDARY GAIN the benefit received from responding to an emotional disturbance in a way which brings a partial satisfaction without resolving the original disturbance

TRANSFERENCE *n.* the passing on of a positive or negative attitude felt in the past towards a parent or other significant person to someone in the present who represents that person

TRAUMA *n.* painful experience that cannot be immediately accepted or mastered

VALENCE *n.* degree of interaction

Subject Index